CHAS AND HIS ROCK 'N' ROLL ALLOTMENT

CHAS AND HIS ROCK 'N' ROLL ALLOTMENT

Chas Hodges

Foreword by Jools Holland OBE

APEX PUBLISHING LTD

Hardback first published in 2010

Apex Publishing Ltd

PO Box 7086, Clacton on Sea, Essex, CO15 5WN, England

www.apexpublishing.co.uk

British Library Cataloguing-in-Publication Data
A catalogue record for this book
is available from the British Library

ISBN HARDBACK: 1-906358-77-X   978-1-906358-77-8

CONTENTS

FOREWORD

I am delighted to be invited to write the foreword to this excellent book.

On checking the gardening section of my library I was disappointed to see how few books there are on the subject of allotments. So it is wonderful to welcome this edition that can at last fill that gap.

It's an illuminating book, written by a great man who has a full understanding of all the pitfalls, the do's and don'ts of allotmenting. The author is a great Londoner who has recognised, like many of the generations before him, the great pleasure that can be gained from seeing nature at work. Especially when it results in creating delicious things we can put on our kitchen table. Indeed the food grown in the London allotment can often be found in the loftiest dining rooms. I happen to know that in Mark's Club, one of London's grandest restaurants, the fruit and veg comes from the headwaiter's allotments. Also, we must remember, that by growing our own veg it's one less trip to the supermarket and therefore a few moments less stress each week. So in short, by having an allotment you can eat like a king, save money, your sanity and the planet.

So when, we ask "How do I go about having an allotment?" Well you are holding the answer in your hands in the form of this useful book. One word of warning would be, that my dear friend Chas often speaks and writes in the vernacular. This means he might, at the drop of a hat, start speaking in traditional Cockney rhyming slang. So please check the context if he refers to apples and pears, syrup of figs, taters, or being a gooseberry, or you might end up with egg all over your boat (see the poultry section in the book).

I wish you many happy hours on your allotment growing food for yourself, family and loved ones whilst at the same time getting away from them all in your potting shed.

Best wishes
Jools Holland OBE

INTRODUCTION

This introduction is mainly to let newcomers to the gardening game (like newly wed husbands, for instance, with young wives who want their families to eat the best) know that gardening and growing your own vegetables can be an enjoyable and fulfilling experience and you still get time to go down the pub for a pint with your mates. Like this gardening book already, don't ya?

I'm speaking from experience. If gardening to you is a chore and a bore and just means keeping the grass cut and dog shit free well read on. I can tell you how it needn't be. Much more than that, it can become something you look forward to doing.

So let's start with the low-maintenance, dog-shit-free lawn and fuck that one off out of it.

Keep pet chickens instead of a pet dog. Pen 'em in a hut on the lawn and you now have a dog-shit-free lawn with no more mowing 'cos the chickens will peck and scratch away, keeping the grass down (they'll eventually get rid of it all together) and you get fresh eggs at the end of it. Ain't that good news?

Of course if you want to keep a dog (I do) then dog turds will have to be dealt with ... somewhere. But that's up to you. Do dog turds annoy you? Does the pleasure of keeping a dog outweigh the task of dog turd duty? This is for you to decide.

Gardening has got everything going for it. For a start it'll keep you fit. Go at it gently, little but often, and you won't have to spend time and money down the gym. Plus you get a bonus in that the food you've grown is being eaten and enjoyed by you and your family.

In the early '70s, when I first started gardening , my

local pub, The Crown in Broxbourne, had on draught a lovely Belgian lager called Lamot. It was in the days when they actually did import the real thing from the Continent - where they brew it best. We know how to brew bitter over here but we ain't no good at lager. (If you should happen to pick up a continental lager that's brewed 'Under Licence in the UK', put it back. Go for British bitter and Continental lager.)

Draught Lamot was lovely. I don't know if it's still around but it was a happy part of my early gardening days. A pleasurable winter's Saturday afternoon digging or a leisurely, languorous summer evening bean-picking was made even more enjoyable when suddenly a pint of Lamot came into my head and I knew I'd be having one down the pub later on.

Another Belgian lager story comes to mind ...

I reckon I was one of the first in England to discover Stella Artois.

I'd been doing a recording session in London and wanted to take a couple of beers home. There in the window of a nearby off-licence was a sign: 'Stella Artois. New Imported Belgian Beer. Special Offer. 2/6 a Bottle.' Now that's how long ago it was. It was in old English money, so I reckon it was around 1971.

2/6 a bottle? 12-and-a-half pence. Cheap for then. But of course it wasn't quite as cheap as 12-and-a-half pence sounds today. Like they say in some books, "All them years ago all I got for a week's work was ten bob!" (50 pence.) "What?" the author wants you to say. "How bad them times were. Working all week and all he takes home is enough to buy a box of matches!" But all them years ago 50 pence, or 10 bob, did buy a little bit more than a box of matches.

My granddad used to say, "Years ago beer was tuppence a pint, and lemonade was a penny." 'What's gone wrong?' I thought. 'Lemonade's sixpence now! They must've had it good in the old days.' Then he would say, but not in the same breath, and not even on the same day, "When I was young, I'd work all week for ten bob."

Hang about. My mate gets more than that for a paper round. Got it! He never said that when he was making me envious of the olden-day cheap lemonade!

I was experiencing my first taste of what old people beef about. One minute how good it was in the old days. Beer was cheap. Next minute, "We had it hard in the old days, not like you lot today, we had to survive on next to nothing."

Old gits. Not my granddad obviously, but all the other granddads. Well, some of 'em. The ones who wouldn't give you your ball back when it went over their garden.

That Stella lager was the best bottled lager I'd ever tasted. I began to seek it out everywhere. It was on a par with Lamot.

But in the meantime disaster went and struck on the Lamot front ...

Draught Lamot was suddenly discontinued in my local pub and the governor didn't know what would replace it. Some dodgy English brewed lager I supposed. But no! In came Stella Artois ... on draught! What a stroke of luck! And it was as good as Lamot, if not better.

So the pleasant post-gardening Belgian pints down the pub resumed once more. Until one night, about six months later ...

I took the first swig of my first pint and lit up my first cigar of the evening. Lovely. The cigar was nice ... but that beer? Was it my imagination? It didn't have that same quality taste. Perhaps it was what I'd eaten for dinner and it was affecting my taste buds? But then I'd eaten what I always ate before going down the pub - six or seven bowls of jellied eels. (Only fucking about ... probably five or six. No, let me be serious. I'd had a tasty 'nothing out of the ordinary' dinner with my wife and kids some two hours earlier.)

Halfway through my first pint it still wasn't giving me pleasant feelings. It wasn't actually bad, but the taste at the back of my throat wasn't a quality one. I did persevere and had a couple more pints. It tasted better after the alcohol had begun to take effect, but that initial pint didn't taste like it used to.

This reminds me a bit of the Jesus story, where he turns the water into wine at the wedding: 'Different qualities of alcohol'. It was his first recorded miracle, but he did fuck it up a bit.

Traditionally the wedding celebrations started off with the best wine and then later, when they were three parts pissed, out came the plonk. They weren't bothered by then. But at this wedding they gave it so much stick that all the wine ran out. Plonk an' all. The guests were beginning to sober up. Jesus's mother was worried, but Jesus said, "Do not worry, mother. I've got an idea that will enable them all to get 'on it' once again. Bring some pitchers of water." And Jesus turned the water into wine.

Now for a start, although this was very pleasing for the equivalent of the lager lout in those days, it hardly benefited mankind. Not only that, he'd been a bit too cocky. He provided them piss artists with top-quality wine instead of plonk, and somebody who was sobering up quicker than the rest sussed.

"How comes we're drinking top-quality wine at this point in the proceedings? One minute we've got fuck all and are gagging for anything, next minute it's 30 BC quality year stuff."

Of course Jesus had to keep his mouth shut. His mum gave him a knowing smile over the top of her glass of claret. He wasn't to know. Poor little fucker. It was his mother's fault. She knew alright. These days he would've been taken into care.

But back to my booze predicament. The draught

Stella wasn't tasting as good. Next thing was, the bottled Stella lager started to taste different. It took on a hard, flinty flavour rather than its usual soft but glorious golden-guzzle flavour.

And then I found out why ...

It was now brewed in Britain.

Once it had started to sell, for economic reasons the Belgians gave the Brits permission to brew it. 'This is okay because the Brits don't know a good lager from a bad one.' And in general there's truth in that. So long as it's strong enough to get pissed on there'll be no complaints. Never mind the quality, add an extra per cent alcohol and that'll take care of that. But no. It ain't good enough for me.

Now I'm going to wander from the plot wildly and talk about tea and coffee. Tea mainly. We are supposed to be a tea-drinking nation. We pride ourselves on the brew. But where can you get real tea? Most of us don't really want Earl Grey. What we want is proper, kettle just boiled, pot pre-warmed, loose-leaved, one generous spoon per cup, builders' tea.

Recently I together with my wife and granddaughter took a train, first class, to Edinburgh. Lovely food in the restaurant car. Then later on we were visited with the tea and coffee flasks. The coffee tasted as if it was brewed from fag ash and the tea ... well, to follow is a quote from one of my old drummers, Don Groom, back in the sixties (remembered now because it has happened so many times):

"The tea was so weak it came out on crutches."

I bet you didn't laugh. Most people don't, but it's a good way of describing it. I think I'm the only one who's ever laughed at that.

But what we are good at is real ale. We brew and serve crap tea, coffee and lager but our real ale is the best. Nobody in the world could do it better. Just imagine Germany or Belgium or France trying to produce real ale? It's the beer only we know how to brew ... but lager?

It's the same with Aussie and American lager. It tastes great when you're drinking their brew of it, but our brew of their brand just ain't no good. I'm rubbing it in now, ain't I?

But all the world's countries have had at least a couple of centuries, and some many more, to perfect their own beer. It has become each country's personal art. It's not a recipe that you can write down and expect someone else to produce with the same result that has taken years to get right. You can teach the notes but you can't teach the feeling.

My last word on this. The Scottish actually don't brew a bad lager - way above the English. But, there again, their ale is a different style to ours. Interesting.

But ain't this supposed to be a gardening book? Yes, but a book to encourage you to grow your own with the incentive of a pint down the pub later. Hence the beer oration. But need I give a reason?!

So, presuming that you've never gardened before – ever ...

Where do you start?

Right!

BASIC TOOLS

A Garden Fork
This is for digging. Obvious? Not really.
Every gardening book I've read recommends a spade for digging.

Dig a trench. Barrow it up to the other end of the plot. Then you fill in that trench with the next line of digging, and then the next line, and so on. In theory you finish at the other end of the plot with a trench that you fill in with the soil you barrowed up there at the beginning. Looks great in the gardening book drawings, but soil don't act like that. When you dig, you don't dig neat breeze-block size chunks like they show in the drawings.

After two-and-a-half rows, the trench has gone - to where you know not - and you're scratching your head wondering where the fuck that pile of soil you barrowed up to the other end is gonna go. I know; I've done it.

Then there's double-digging (look it up somewhere else), described in the books. Frightening. It must go on and I ain't saying that it ain't a good idea, but in my 40 years of gardening I've never known anyone who's done it. So at best it's a pretty obscure type of crap soil that needs this treatment.

I think - in fact I'm certain - that a lot of these gardening books are required by their publisher to be, say, 50,000 words long. So they've got to 30,000 words and they've finished. Now what the fuck are they gonna do? They're more bothered about the advance than the content, so the rest is filled up with crap.

But that don't happen with me. I play the piano for a living.

So that's the double-digging and the spade-trenching fucked off out of it.

Let's get back to the fork.

Buy a men's garden fork if you're a man, and a ladies' garden fork if you're a lady. The ladies' fork is slightly smaller but actually does just as good a job.

When I got better from being old (over-imbibing) a few years ago, I got back into gardening with a ladies' fork. It ain't nothin' to be ashamed of. I've worn my wife's knickers sometimes ... only when there were no pants at hand. I've got a real man's fork now ... but there are still times I go short of pants.

Every gardener I've ever come into contact with has used a fork to dig over his plot. Experience has taught us that the biggest bane, especially on a newly acquired neglected allotment plot, is couch grass, or twitch grass. It has roots like spaghetti that spread. If digging with a fork the roots are relatively easy to remove, but you must be meticulous. And don't compost 'em. Put 'em on a bonfire. Or, as on my allotment, you can spread them on worn-out grass paths. If they take root there, which they don't, it don't matter.

I tried digging with a spade one year - an American spade. I bought it in Cleveland, Ohio, on a Chas and Dave trip and had it flown back home. It got lost in Chicago and arrived at my home a week later by special courier. It was well wrapped up and the delivery man thought it was some sort or rare guitar I'd bought in America. He laughed when I said it was a spade. He didn't believe me. So I left him to pass on the story to his mates.

I found out that this type of spade originated in Ireland. It's got a long handle and the metal spade has a pointed tip.

It is the loveliest spade for digging and if you are up for trenching or double-digging then this is the spade for you. The leverage of the long handle makes it so

8

pleasant to use.

However, if you've got twitch grass a spade just chops up the mass of roots into loads of little bits that all grow shoots, so creating a nightmare. So use a fork to loosen the sods and you can drag out long pieces of the root as you go.

A Dutch Hoe

This is your next most important tool. I carry mine around with me all the time when I'm on the allotment. Keep the hoe going at all times between the rows you've sown, skimming it across the top of the soil and chopping the heads off anything you don't want coming up. It's a most pleasant thing to do. Even hoe when you can't see growth 'cos it'll help stop it starting.

It's strange that a weak person is called a 'weed'. Ignore one and it'll take over your garden.

A Trowel

A small shovel for digging a small hole to drop a potato in, or a smaller hole to drop an onion set in. (You'll read about these later on - tiny onions about half an inch across, onion sets, that you plant just below the surface around March time.)

A Rake

This is a sort of tidying tool that also transforms your soil to a fine tilth (a crumb-like finish) ready for seed sowing. General fucking about with a rake gets your plot looking neat.

Look at the lumpy soil, then look at the rake. You'll get the idea as to what needs to be done and how to use it.

A Strimmer

A luxury tool, but very handy if you can afford one. They can be petrol-driven or electric. It's a sort of power-driven scythe, only it's not shaped like one (see illustration). It does the same job, only quicker. It's very handy for cutting short the grass paths around your plot that you've only just noticed are beginning to look like a jungle.

Sticks and String

Two sharp sticks and a length of string that will span your plot. When seed sowing this sets out a measured distance between rows and guides you towards a nice straight row.

A Swan-necked Hoe

Used for 'earthing up'; trying, in fact, to bury the plant you are growing, such as potato, leek or celery. You drag earth up to the plant from each side. This keeps the light from it and blanches it to enhance the delicate flavour in general. This tool does the job well.

As you get more into it you'll discover more tools and will start saying things like, "Yeah! One of them would be good. I'll get one tomorrow." And it might be good … but it might also be something you'll use once and then never use again. I'm gonna leave that decision up to you. The above tools I reckon are all you really need. The rest are a luxury - but then why not, if now and again you can afford it? It's all part of the fun.

CHASSIE'S ROCK 'N' ROLL ALLOTMENT

I first really got into growing my own in the spring of 1972. Me, Joan and the kids (Juliet aged 5 and Kate aged 1) moved into a little bungalow in Broxbourne (Nik was born there in 1974, he plays drums for me now). The bungalow had been lived in since the turn of the century by two sisters, Glad and Grace. They were born in the latter part of the Victorian age and were now well into their seventies. We had bought it from them and the two of them now lived in the bigger house next door.

Coming from a tower block in Edmonton, it was like acquiring our own piece of heaven. It had a 200-foot long garden; in Edmonton we only had a concrete balcony, 22 floors up. So can you imagine how we all felt? To Kate, our youngest, it must have really seemed like a new world, with grass and worms and birds and butterflies suddenly all around her.

The garden had been kept in old-style, immaculate, wartime, proper food produce manner, with three apple trees at the end - two cooking apple trees and one eater. By the house was a plot of the finest soil you could ever wish for. Glad and Grace were gardeners and the soil condition was down to their good husbandry (care and cultivation of the land) over the years. I've always regarded that soil as a paragon and I've used it as a yardstick when working on any soil I've had since.

I've had my current allotment plot for almost ten years. With manuring, digging and raking between gigs, some seasons I managed to get it pretty close to that old Broxbourne plot.

It's very stony though, which the old Broxbourne plot wasn't. Although stony ground drains off easily and never gets waterlogged, it means that deep-reaching root vegetables such as parsnips and regular carrots easily become 'forked'. That is, the 'taproot', the single main root that begins to form soon after germination, on encountering an obstruction, e.g. a stone, splits itself into two on the way down and continues to do so on meeting similar obstacles, multiplying as it goes. Everything can look great on top, but dig up what looks like a nice carrot or parsnip and you find instead of one root you have several spindly roots. You can fiddle about and still cook them, but a single, nice fat root would be better, if you can get it. And you can on stony ground. I've done it. It works.

The carrots I like to grow are Van Hage's 'Flak' variety. These eventually grow to the size of a parsnip, if not bigger. They can be three inches in diameter and a foot or more deep - and beyond that if you fancy nurturing them into prize winners. But the small 'thinnings' that you pull as they grow are of top-quality flavour.

This method works for me for both parsnips and carrots.

Get an iron spike and a hammer (I borrow the poker from the fireplace). Knock the spike into the soil about a foot deep and then twizzle it around to make a cone-shaped hole about four inches or so across. Fill the hole with John Innes Seed Sowing Compost and sow a small pinch of seeds in the middle of it. Thin to the strongest one when the seedlings are about an inch high.

How deep should you sow the seeds? A good general rule for any seed sowing is to go by the size of the seed and sow it to the same depth. Carrot seeds are tiny and parsnip seeds are flat. Sow these on top of the soil, around every six inches in rows spaced around two feet apart. As they grow to eatable size pull every other one, leaving the rest to grow on at a foot apart.

Good luck with carrot fly. Gardening books suggest many things you can try, but this rock 'n' roller in between gigs digs the carrot, cuts out any black bits left by the carrot fly, and leaves the clean, prepared bits in the fridge in a polythene bag ready for the next dinner. (Carrot fly are a nuisance but in my experience not enough to render the carrot totally fucked.)

The last time I gave a bagful to Dave, he swore he'd never tasted carrots like that since he was a kid, and Dave has always been an honest critic.

Try to keep carrots well watered (little and often). If you don't, a heavy rainfall after a dry period will cause them to split. They can of course still be eaten but they won't win no prizes and there'll be a lot of waste carrot to cut away.

Now, no matter what you do in life, there's gonna be someone out there ready to tell you you're doing it wrong: "That ain't the right way, you should do it this way," etc.

In no way at all am I saying that my way is the best. It's simply how I've done it - things I've tried that have worked; things I've tried that haven't worked. But everything I'm writing about in this book I have tried and I'm giving you my conclusions from my own experiences. Anything that I haven't tried I'll recommend that you find out from elsewhere. In general, however, I ain't done too bad.

I've often read gardening books (and cookery books) and have been suspicious that the author hasn't actually done all of it. I heard some gardeners talking on the radio the other day (and they skim over it): "Oh yes, of course we've all done that. Stick three cocktail sticks in an avocado pear stone, suspend it over a jar of water (or whatever) and watch it burst into life" - but have you?

Hang on a minute! I heard talk about this some years

ago. What a good idea! I thought. So I tried it. Nothing happened. I tried it again. Nothing. And I ain't no slouch in the Amateur Gardening Brigade. Have they done it? Or have they just heard about it? I've done the 'three cocktail stick' trick on the avocado stones loads of times, then stuck 'em in various occupied house plant pots, given 'em pots of their own and placed 'em in plots of their own. Result? Fuck all!

If you do the same with a spare garlic clove - stick it in a plant pot, balance it on top of a coke bottle filled with water - away it goes. It does you proud. It just loves to please. But avocado stones just sit there and refuse to budge. They just don't want to know.

I'm going to put this one to *Gardeners' Question Time* on BBC Radio 4 before this book goes to print. I'll put their answer at the foot of this page.*

I would like to have success with these stones. They're so solid and sturdy; too nice to chuck away.

But in the meantime I'll get back to growing stuff that I've found does work ...

* *Answer: Well, I've e-mailed 'em twice and sent a hand written letter. That was over three months ago. No answer. Thought as much, they're having me on. No one's actually done it.*

ONIONS

I love 'em and they are easy to grow.

I first learned what 'onion sets' were from Glad and Grace. I learned a lot from them. They'd had the wartime food-growing experience. What better?

'Onion sets' are baby onions, usually around half an inch across, that are grown from seed the season before. You can get them from garden centres and they can be set (planted) in the autumn or spring. Autumn sets will mature earlier, but I was told by an allotment mate only last week that they don't keep so well. I don't know about that. I usually put them out in the spring, around the beginning of March, and they keep alright.

Go by what you like the look of on the packet. You won't go far wrong with any of them, as they're all pretty good.

So I set them early March. Push them just below the soil (or dig a tiny hole if the soil's a bit hard) six inches apart and leaving about eighteen inches between the rows. Eventually, when fat spring onion size, you can start pulling them up to eat. Lovely. Take out every other one and leave the rest to grow on and mature. Keep the soil well weeded. Little and often will stop weeds from taking hold.

Around June/July time the green tops will begin to turn to a dry yellow 'straw'. Pull them up and leave them on the soil to dry out for a couple of days. Make sure the roots are facing south so they get the maximum amount of sun for root drying.

Then it's time to store them. They must have air around them to store well. Glad and Grace used to bundle them up in bunches of six and hang them in the barn (or garage). Do this and they will keep to the last onion.

It is so worth growing onions from sets, especially if, like me, you like raw onions. No shop onion has got the crunchy, juicy nuttiness of a freshly pulled or garage-stored set onion. And when you pull 'em do your nose a favour and smell the root. Fresh earth mingled with fresh pulled onion root - what a treat for the hooter! You won't experience that unless you grow your own.

Chop it up and eat it with whatever you want. Then put the rest in a jam jar with vinegar and pepper and dip into this daily. My granddaughter Charlie loves 'em this style.

SHALLOTS

Shallot sets can be bought and planted in the same way as onion sets, but each bulb, instead of producing a bigger bulb, will multiply into several bulbs.

When you see a nice bunch of green shoots getting on for a foot high pull them (every other one) and you get yourself a nice bunch of salad onions. Eat the whole lot apart from the very tips, which start to go straw-like.

The ones you leave to mature (in the same way as ordinary onion sets) will produce bullet-hard onions for pickling.

My granddaughter Charlie says I must document my pickled onion recipe.

A few years ago, after a shopping day when Charlie was about six, she'd gone with her mum and Joan to a fish and chip restaurant. Charlie ordered pickled onions with hers. It was her first shop-bought pickled onion.

One bite and, "They ain't a patch on granddads!" was the verdict. So here's how I do 'em …

PICKLED ONIONS

Don't buy the ready-spiced pickling vinegar they sell in the shops. I don't know why, but it hasn't got the flavour. It's much better to make your own spiced vinegar.

Buy a packet of pickling spice and empty one of the sachets into a saucepan with a pint of vinegar. Put it on the simmering plate if you've got an Aga. If you haven't got one, move heaven and earth to get yourself one.

Every house should have a piano and an Aga. And of course they both should be used constantly. I've been in houses where they have an Aga and been informed: "Of course we don't use it. We have the latest digital electronic cooker that just does everything. It even wipes the baby's arse after it's cooked your Sunday dinner and you can get Radio Luxembourg on it." (Only people around my age will get that last bit. I was born in 1943. Show this paragraph to anyone born in the war in fact. Their eyes will smile and will tell you what I'm on about.)

So, you must have an Aga (that you use) and a piano.

I've been round people's houses that proudly exhibit gleaming pianos, with a vase of flowers on top! I won't allow anything that contains liquid to be put on top of the piano - absolute disaster if it gets knocked over.

We did the Alan Titchmarsh show not long ago and they set us up with beers on the piano. I asked nicely for them to be removed. They did so nicely. I don't know whose idea it was. Probably his - ol' sharks' eyes.

Then these same people who think a piano should be used like a sideboard say, "I keep it locked, of course, so the kids can't bang on it."

Let the kids bang on it for fuck's sake! That's what a piano wants. It needs its moving parts to be kept in motion regularly, like us. Let 'em bang on it – with one golden rule: they only use their hands; no Dinky Toys or table tennis bats.

All my kids as soon as, in their high chairs, were pushed up to the piano to have fun and 'bang away'. They've all ended up good piano players.

Back to pickled onions ...

So, you've emptied a sachet of pickling spice into a saucepan with a pint of vinegar.

To the vinegar in the saucepan add a 'visual' half-inch of water (roughly). Simmer the vinegar and pickling spice down until it reaches the original level or thereabouts. Then you're back to pure vinegar, but it's now nicely spiced.

Leave it to cool and then strain it and put it in a jar.

In fact I've done this back to front, but it don't matter. The spiced vinegar will keep until we've done the onions.

Pickling Onions and Shallots

They need soaking for 24 hours in salt water. Use about a tablespoon of salt to four pints of water. Don't bother peeling or preparing them, just put them, skins an' all, into the salt water. The next day, after you've topped and tailed 'em, the outer brown skin will just peel off nicely with minimal waste. Fill your jars with the onions and eke out the spiced vinegar in each jar. Top up with plain malt vinegar.

Now, unlike pickled cabbage (which I'll get to later), the longer you keep them the crisper they get. But this ain't always possible.

Years ago, before I achieved a bit better willpower, I used to get my wife to hide the Christmas pickled onions I'd done and get her to promise, however much I begged and pleaded, not to let me know where they were. I'd keep a small jar for immediate consumption and then waited, craving for the full Onion Club payout at Christmas.

I found some things while searching for them though: that puncture outfit I lost last summer, behind the disused outside toilet; and a banjo vellum stuffed up the chimney - now who would've done that? I suppose it was me. I remember buying it. But perhaps it was a clever ploy? If I'd reached past the vellum I would've found the onions! I only just thought of that. Why didn't I think of it before? She knew I'd be so happy finding that vellum that I would look no further. Of course it was a ploy. Why would I put a banjo vellum up the chimney? I don't go around doing things like that ... I'm too young.

Before I leave the subject of pickled onions, I wanna tell you a story of me and Dave's little mate Brian. We met him in a pub near Ware some years ago.

Brian would come out with some of the greatest witty lines, which would have the whole pub falling about. But he didn't know he was delivering them. For instance, someone came in the pub one evening and noticed there was a bit of stubble on Brian's upper lip:

"So you're growing a moustache are you, Brian?"

"Who fuckin' told you? That was supposed to be a surprise for my mum!"

And the day I saw him in the pub one snowy dinnertime, when he should've been working in the hotel next door as general hotel ground tidy upper:

"Why ain't you next door, Brian?"

"They want me outside clearing snow!"

"Well that's alright, ain't it?"

"I ain't going out clearing snow in this weather!"

Then you laugh and he looks at you blankly, not even wondering, 'what's funny in that?'

I was giving him a lift home one night. We were a few yards from his house when we had to slow down because the car in front was crawling a bit. It didn't bother me because we were in no hurry, but the car kindly pulled over to let us pass.

"Stop!" said Brian, "I know him."

So I did. We pulled alongside and Brian wound the window down.

"You dozy cunt!" said Brian. "Holding all the traffic up! You should be banned from driving!"

He wound the window back up, laughing. "That's told him!" said Brian.

"Who's that?" I asked, thinking it was one of his neighbour herberts.

"It's the vicar. Vicar Johnson. He's as blind as a fuckin' bat. My dad reckons he should be banned."

So that's Brian.

So how does he fit into the 'pickled onion' chapter? Well, here we go.

This particular year was a good one for onions and I'd managed to pickle a few extra jars of shallots. It was getting near Christmas, so I said to Brian, "D'ya want a jar of my pickled onions?" "Love some, mate!" So I took them up the pub for him and he took them home.

Sitting with him in the pub in January of the New Year I said to him, "By the way, Brian, how did them pickled onions go down over Christmas?"

"Lovely, mate. They really done the trick!" said Brian.

I was pleased. "So did you have 'em with your Boxing Day turkey?" I said, pursuing the conversation. I always make sure I do that with Brian. He's one of the few people I always prompt to keep on rabbiting, as I know sooner or later with encouragement he'll come out with something that will astound you and double you up. I wasn't about to be disappointed.

"No, mate." said Brian.

"So when did you eat 'em?"

"We didn't," said Brian.

"But you said they done the trick?"

"They did! We've been having trouble with our cats

21

pissing on the carpet. Mum said that putting pickled onions round 'em puts 'em off doing it. We put 'em all round the carpet and not one cat pissed on it. I'll have another jar of them when they're available."

My top quality, none better, organically grown and perfectly pickled onions reduced to cat piss stoppers! But it was a compliment as far as Brian was concerned.

We took him to Southend one year. On the way home he was a bit quiet. I think he was about to nod off, but I wanted him to talk. His mum's got a lot of cats. Brian likes cats. I'll prompt him into a cat conversation.

"How's the cats, Brian?"

He stirred from his imminent snooze. "Well they're alright now. Well Spiffy is."

"What do you mean?"

" Spiffy's alright now."

"Why? What was wrong?"

Still not fully awake. "Trod on his fuckin' head, didn't I?"

After the initial impact - us all with massive laughter stitch pains - we began to recover.

"How comes?"

"I've come running down the stairs and Spiffy's dozing on the bottom step, like, y'know. I didn't see him and trod on his fuckin' head. I thought 'Oh no! What have I fuckin' done now?' [Brian is a bit hefty.] Spiffy squawked and run into the kitchen."

"What happened next?"

"It cost 200 fuckin' quid to get his jaw fixed. Mum's taking it out of my allowance."

Brian's got continual, ongoing cat stories that I always try to get out of him. Another one comes to mind.

"How's the cats?"

"Alright, mate."

"Behaving theirselves?"

"Yeah, yeah ... Well, kind of, mate."

"Kind of what?"

"Well, Tompy pissed in dad's dinner last night."

We fell about. Not a crack of emotion either way on Brian's face.

"So, how come?"

"Dad was eating his dinner and Tompy jumped up on the table. He started dobbing his back feet up and down, like, one after the other, y'know, and before dad could do anything his tail started juddering and he pissed in his dinner. Dad said, 'Fucking cat' and threw him across the room. Didn't hurt him though. He landed on his feet in his basket."

There are bound to be more 'Brian stories' in this book, but I'll eke 'em out when the timing's right.

It'll be worth the wait.

CHRISTMAS TIME AND TURKEYS

While we're on the subject of Christmas fayre, me and my brother Dave, him of 'No Pleasin' You' inspiration …

But did I ever tell you that? It was his missus's remark, "Them curtains you're putting up ain't straight," and his catchy retort, "There ain't no fuckin' pleasin' you is there?" that inspired me to write it.

… well, we hit on a plan we thought was infallible for the perfect Christmas turkey.

We both fancied the idea of buying a young turkey and fattening it up for Christmas. But neither of us could face the idea of giving it the chop after we'd got to know it.

Then I hit on a solution. I said, "We can rear each other's turkeys! You fatten my one up and I fatten up yours and we'll swap 'em over at Christmas! Then we'll both be eating strangers, so no emotions."

Just to dwell on that for a moment - 'Eating Strangers' sounds like a good title for an autobiography of a cannibal.

I wonder if cannibals ever had any foibles about eating people they knew or relatives? Would they, for instance, eat Uncle George? He died natural. He fell out of a tree.

So would they say, "We all know Uncle George ate healthy. Not a lot of red meat and mostly fresh fruit and vegetables. Plenty good nosebag."

Or would they say, "No, let's give him a proper funeral," then all go back to the house and eat someone else?

Don't know.

But then my turkey swap idea with the brother began to get complicated.

"How will I know if you're feeding mine properly?" said the brother.

"Well of course I will," I said. "I know how to rear poultry!"

"But I want him to have the best. How am I gonna be sure?"

"Hang about!" I interrupted smartly. "How am I gonna know you're keeping mine in good shape?"

"True."

"Hold up. I've got it!" I said. "We both go and choose the feed, buy the lot and split the feed down the middle."

"Perfect!" he said. "But [here we go ...] "you don't get out of bed till the afternoon. My turkey's gonna be starving. Your turkey will be alright. He'll get fed at 7 in the morning before I go to work."

I knew it! It always did get up his nose, me not having a proper job - out gigging, going to bed late and getting up late.

"I also think," said the brother, "that we should have reasonable access to each other's turkeys, say every Saturday afternoon, so's we can both check on the progress of the fattening up of each other's birds."

"But that will defeat the whole object of the plan," I said. "We'll get to know our birds. 'How are you?' and all that. 'Is he feeding you well? Never mind, you'll soon be home and on the table in time for Christmas.'"

No! This ain't going to work!

Actually, most of the last paragraph didn't really happen. It's what me and my brother visualised and laughed about after I suggested the idea. We both came up with these probable scenarios of going round each other's houses, checking on the general fatness of each other's turkey.

We could also picture Boxing Day. We'd meet in the

pub.

"What was the turkey like then, Dave?"

"The breast was alright but the legs were a bit tough. You must've let it run around a lot?"

"What do you mean by that? What else does a free-range turkey do? You can't tell him to take it easy, go rest your legs 'cos they'll toughen up if you're not careful and won't make good eating."

"You're being daft now. I made sure your one got proper exercise but didn't go mad. I bet it was that dog of yours, chasing him all around the yard all the time. The meat in them legs was as tough as catapult elastic."

"Okay. Now we're on the subject, mine certainly hadn't been exactly 'corn fed'. The whole bird was as dry as a bone. A plate of mashed cocktail sticks would've been tastier. Just what did you feed him on?"

"Proper organic food that my wife cooked."

"Leftovers."

"Yes, if you like. So what's wrong with that?"

"Left over 'cos neither one of you could eat it. Slops, if you like! So you gave it to my turkey!"

And so on!

We had fun with the idea, but there was only one way for everyone to be happy: let the wives deal with the Christmas turkeys.

Now we're doin' the turkey trot, here's another Christmas turkey story.

In the early '60s, me, mum, stepfather Irish John, brother Dave and sister Jean all lived together at home in Edmonton.

We'd never ever had turkey for Christmas; that was well out of our league. So we'd have chicken. But even chicken was expensive. It really was. It was more expensive than beef or pork or lamb. Then suddenly they started selling it in fish and chip shops for the same price as a portion of fish 'n' chips. Great!

I found out later that chicken suddenly got cheap because of this 'wonderful new idea' of battery farms. Hens were made to lay eggs for a year and then sold off for meat. The meat was nice and tender, especially the legs, because the animal never had chance to use them. The wings were nice and tender too; no room to exercise them. The cage it lived in was about a foot square. Today, at last, they are beginning to do away with this practice.

On Christmas Eve around 1962, under the covered market in Edmonton, some bright 'Del Boy' hit on the idea of an all-day turkey auction and it proved to be a winner all round. Punters would come and go throughout the day. Well, it was a sort of auction. Come to think of it, it wasn't really an auction at all; it was just clever 'wide boy' selling - the type of selling they do on TV today. That's where it came from originally:

"Now, not only a seasoned Moroccan mahogany chopping board at only 30 pounds, but a set of South Sheffield chopping knives in a real cow leather carrying case and a Swiss army knife sharpener thrown in. All for the same price!"

Only in the market it would be:

"Now, not only a natural fattened English country turkey at a mere thirty bob, but a hand-turned Pymmes Park cedar turkey prodder in a classy Hackney hessian pouch, plus half a pound of Paxo. All for the same price. And, 'ere you are lady, at my expense, and I barely make a profit, a Ronson pot scourer thrown in!"

It was the place to buy your turkey. You loved the banter and you always got a bargain. You didn't mind that the turkey prodder was a wooden Woolworths spoon wrapped in a bit of sacking. It didn't matter. You were going home with a turkey for Christmas.

And in those days there were not many houses down our street that had a turkey in the oven on Christmas morning.

So on Christmas Eve 1962, with some nice Christmas gig money in my pocket, I decided I was going to take home our first ever Christmas turkey. I hit it just right. I can't remember how much I paid, but I got it at a good price. I arrived home in the early evening and plonked it on the front room table.

"Look what I got, mum! Got it under the covered market!"

"Ooh, lovely!" said mum. "I'll put it in the larder."

Twenty minutes later we heard the front door go and in comes brother Dave.

"Look what I got mum! Got it under the covered market!" Another turkey.

"Ooh, lovely!" said mum, winking at me. "I'll put it in the larder."

Then the front door goes again. It's the stepfather, Irish John.

"Look what I got, Daiz!"

"GOT IT UNDER THE COVERED MARKET?" we all said.

John looked confused.

"That's two we've got!" said Dave.

"No it ain't, it's three!" I piped up.

All three got cooked. We were still eating turkey the following Easter, or it seemed like we were anyway. Everything tasted of turkey for months after - even Easter eggs.

MAMMOTH ONIONS

Here's what you do if you want to grow enormous ones. Tasty too. I've tried it for three years, but not running; twice in the '70s (won a prize in the local show, St Giles Hall, Nazeing) and I grew 'em again a few years back. I took 'em on Ready, Steady, Cook! and Ainsley Harriott was impressed.

In 1972 an old boy in my local pub, The Crown in Broxbourne, told me how to grow 'em.

These onions are not grown from 'sets' but from seed. The best seed to get is 'Robinson's Mammoth', which you can get by mail order. Give 'em space when you finally plant them out, as they can grow to the size of a junior football.

The old boy told me I must sow the onion seed on the shortest day of the year, which is usually 21st or 22nd December, the eve of their natural germination day. Make a note in your diary or you'll forget. That's why I've only grown them three times in 30-odd years. When I get the normal springtime sowing feelings, it's too late for them. (Must make a note in new diary!) They can be sown in a propagator or in a tray, and then put in a greenhouse with a little heat underneath. A slow-going paraffin heater, just to take the chill out of the air, will suffice and it's most economical. Sow thinly. I sow them indoors while listening to a radio play. (I record them on tape all the time. It's a great pre-Christmas twilight-zone thing to do. Must do them this year.)

I sow the seed with tweezers an inch apart in a 12-inch by 6-inch seed tray in John Innes seed-sowing compost. It saves thinning them out and is a pleasant, relaxing task.

When the seedlings begin to show, water the tray (if the soil looks dry) by placing it in the kitchen sink with the plug in and running the cold tap until the water almost reaches the rim of the tray. Leave it for a few seconds and the water will begin to show on the surface of the soil. Lift it and let it drain on the draining board. Watering this way won't disturb the delicate seedlings. Do this whenever the soil begins to look dry.

Don't overwater. A waterlogged tray or pot will rot the seeds or roots.

A good test, which can be used for any container plants (do this to all your indoor plants), is to stick your finger in the edge of the pot or tray. If your finger comes out with soil stuck to it, it don't need water. If your finger comes out dry, it does.

When the onions are around small knitting needle size, a bit thicker than spaghetti, they are ready to be planted out into the open ground.

Plant the seedlings 12 inches apart in rows 18 inches apart. Keep well weeded, little but often, and away they'll go.

Gardening has to be part of your day along with your food and drink. Plan yourself a regular time if yours is a routine-based, orderly world; just after breakfast, or just back from work, or whatever. Enjoy wandering around, weeding, doing little things that catch your eye for 20 or 30 minutes. Linger longer if you want, but do it daily. If yours ain't an orderly world, like mine, always think 'gardening'. Then, when there's some unexpected time to spare, get out and 'garden'.

If it's raining, I play the piano. If it's raining, you could learn to play the piano if you don't play it already. Age, by the way, if you're getting on a bit, don't come into it. Someone I know who was 65 said, "It ain't worth me learning the piano at my age. I'm gonna be 70 before I can say 'I can really play the piano'." So, okay, what would you rather be? A 70-year-old who can't play the piano, or a 70-year-old who can?

Being close to the earth gives you an enormous amount of pleasure and a feeling of well being. Don't get out of the habit. It's easily done, but you'll miss a lot. Other habits can begin to take over and it can happen that you won't actually realise what you are missing. But your head won't feel as good.

No, don't let it slip. Let it become part of your day and life. Once you do you'll wonder what you ever did without it. It mixes so well with whatever your job is. And whatever your job is, it will be the better for it.

Like everyone, gardeners talk about the weather. But a close second is weeds. Root out the perennials (the weeds that have permanent roots, so come up every year) and keep that hoe in your hand at all times, chopping the heads off the annuals (which are the weeds that are pretty shallow rooted but rely on spreading the annual word by way of seed). Get 'em as soon as you see 'em and they won't get a chance to go to seed.

'One year's seeding, seven years weeding.' Good adage.

As a general rule, don't try pulling that perennial out. It will just break off, leaving the tough root in the ground. Dig that root out and it won't come up next year.

If in doubt as to whether they're perennial or annual, just keep chopping the heads off all the gits with the Dutch hoe and eventually they'll get so fed up with it they'll give up.

Deal with weeds 'little and often' and they won't take over.

Weeds growing on your plot is actually a good sign. As another old gardener once said to me, "If weeds don't grow on your ground, son, you're in trouble. There's something seriously wrong with your soil."

My lifestyle constantly sends me here, there and everywhere, but I'm back to the soil as soon as, putting the unavoidable neglect back in shape. And, bit by bit, it's looking a million dollars again.

Sorry, I sort of deviated. So what's next with the old boy's Mammoth Onions?

Right. We're at the stage where the onions seedlings are all planted out. They will grow and grow, the old sage assured me (and he was right) throughout the summer until the longest day - usually 21st or 22nd June. After that day they will begin to ripen off.

When the tops have almost died back, pull them and lay these mini-footballs on the ground, again leaving the roots facing south for maximum drying, for two or three days. Then store them as for set-grown onions, bunched up and hung in a barn or garage.

I gave a couple to Dave years ago. He left them in his barn and when he took them in he noticed fingernail marks on them. His old gardener had never seen onions that size before and thought they were plastic! Hence the fingernail test.

The last time I grew 'em was three years ago. Writing about them here has given me the buzz again. They're on my list for this year.

Now for that pickled cabbage I said I'd get to later …

I don't grow brassicas (the cabbage family) on my Rock 'n' Roll Allotment, the reason being that slugs like 'em, caterpillars like 'em and pigeons like 'em. I'd sooner grow more sweetcorn or onions or beetroot, which in my experience have proved to be completely pest and disease free.

So I buy a red cabbage to pickle. Chop it up, put it through the salad spinner to rid it of mustiness and put it straight into a big jar of my own spiced vinegar. (See 'Pickled Onions'). Don't bother pre-salting it; it ain't gonna last long. Start eating it after two or three days. Eat it with everything, especially your breakfast egg and bacon. It's lovely.

When I do it, I do an extra jar for Dave's sister, Marie. She goes into raptures over it. She's a good judge. Do it yourself. It's so easy. You'll never buy the shop stuff again.

My family all loved gardening, especially on my mum's side - the Tylers. (In my early musician days I toyed with the idea of changing my professional name to 'Chas Tyler', but while I was deciding, 'Hodges' began getting printed on record covers and in odd teen magazines so I went with the flow. But I still think 'Chas Tyler' has a nice ring about it.)

Uncle Alf Tyler, mum's brother, was a good gardener. He had a big peach tree in his garden in Navarino Road, Hackney, which he grew himself. He'd bought an expensive peach during the war and planted the stone. I don't know how long the tree took to come to fruition, but I remember him giving me some to take home to mum in the '60s. He sure got his money back on that one.

In the '70s, when I first got into serious gardening, I grew from seed some nice plum tomato plants. The variety was 'Roma'. If you see 'em, give 'em a go. I can smell 'em frying now. They're lovely. They're more meaty than juicy, so perfect for frying or stewing. They don't reduce down to nothing.

I gave a dozen plants to my Uncle Alf, and here comes an interesting thing that I've never got to the bottom of. The next time I went round to see him, he took me out to his garden. Half of the plants I'd given him were thriving, and half were withering and obviously on their way out. Then he pointed out that six had been tethered to their canes with sisal string and six with nylon string. The ones tethered with nylon string were those that were dying. It was that shiny light green nylon twine that you still see today.

To this day I always tie tomatoes with sisal string. I

never use nylon twine even though I can't figure out how it would affect the plant in such a way. But there it was. Every plant that was tied with that nylon twine died.

So I ain't taking no chances and in blight-free years I've always had a good crop. But it's a strange one, ain't it?

Uncle Alf's heart was more into growing flowers, most of which he grew from seed.

He said to me one day, "I like experimenting with pansies."

I couldn't resist it. "You'll get into trouble doing that, Uncle Alf!" I said.

He was quick. He promised not to do it anymore.

LEEKS

Leeks are another lovely vegetable to grow. They taste like a cross between a nice onion and a swede or cabbage.

As well as the taste, a big attraction for growing leeks is that it's one of the few vegetables that you can harvest in the winter. They will sit there happily all through winter, come hail or snow. They can be eaten raw or cooked, and you can eat the whole lot if you want, leaves and all, if they look in good shape.

As they are very onion-like, treat the sowing and growing similarly, except they don't need to be sown until March, so they don't need artificial heat.

Sow 'em in a seed tray, in the same way, listening to a radio play. (I've accidentally made a start to a poem. Finish it off if you want.) Only this time, when planting them out into the open ground, the method is slightly different.

Sow in March (method as per Mammoth onions, earlier in this book) and they'll be ready to be planted out by June when they'll be around pencil thick.

Water the tray well and gently separate each leek. (Smell the roots. They're lovely!) Then trim the top growth by about a quarter and the root growth by about half.

Plant out, spacing as for 'Mammoth Onions' (well, nine inches apart will do), but this time just dib a hole about half the length of the plant. Drop the plant into the hole and top the hole up with water. And that's it. Earth 'em up gradual as they start to grow, with a swan-necked hoe. (If you're stuck for a last line on the poem, you can have the last sentence.)

Now that's got me into song-writing mode.

"Earth 'em up gradual, as they start to grow.

Earth 'em up gradual, with a swan-necked hoe."

As I said, this is a lovely winter vegetable that can stay put until you want it - all winter long until spring - then it will start to go to seed.

(I'm going to take a break here. I gotta song on my mind. This 'Earth 'em up gradual' could have something.)

No, fuck all with that one. Well, at the moment anyway. Bit too Alan Titchmarsh. But wait …

"Earth 'em up gradual" … But something else comes to mind:

Titchmarsh likes to go on the river, messing about on a punt.

My head's gone. It's so nearly there. I've got to own up. I'm stumped for a rhyme. Oh well, it happens.

There are other winter vegetables if you want to venture into that area: Brussels sprouts, kale and other brassicas (cabbage family, e.g. cauliflower, khol rabi). But I'm only telling you what suits me as a rock 'n' roll gardener. Pigeons love brassicas. Unless they're protected by secure cages or nets, they will move in like biblical locusts to give massive stick to your crop. If they're seedlings they'll eat the fucking lot.

Spinach is a great alternative to brassica winter greens. Neither pigeons nor slugs seem to like it, which is handy, so it will grow uncovered and untroubled. A real rock 'n' roll cropper. It's lovely raw as a change from lettuce. To cook, don't add water. Just wash the leaves, add olive oil or butter and cook over a gentle heat, stirring all the time. Add garlic, as my Italian mate Vito over the allotment does, and it's lovely. As soon as it looks cooked, it is.

Garlic is well worth growing too. The cloves won't grow as fat as the Continental ones you get in the supermarket, but they'll be juicier. And of course you don't use 'em in the same quantity as you do onions, so you don't need to grow so many.

Plant 'em at the end of the season and they'll get a good root system. Around October onwards the days begin to get colder, but the soil still retains its summer warmth for a while. The garlic loves to get its toes nice and comfortably settled in this before the real English bone-freezing weather sets in, which still comes around to prove that global warming ain't all it's cracked up to be.

So plant them in October. Buy your garlic from a supermarket - the ordinary culinary kind. It's cheaper and just as good and you can get organic now. Separate the cloves and plant them like onion sets, only this time a couple of inches beneath the ground and 6 inches apart, leaving the usual 18 inches between rows.

They'll start to ripen off in early summer the following year. Don't leave 'em too long after the tops have died down, 'cos the tops will go to nothing and you'll forget where you put 'em. When you dig 'em you'll find that, like shallots, they have multiplied themselves, only beneath the ground.

Treat and store 'em like onions.

IN DEFENCE OF
OUR WEATHER

Our weather is notorious all around the globe. Cold, wet winters and slightly warmer, wet summers.

A bit of an unfair judgement really considering we always seem to get a hosepipe ban at some point most summers.

But, whatever, I love rain. It makes me feel good and rain haters get right up my snout. If they don't like it then that's their choice, but when they presume that you don't like it too I think they've got a fucking cheek.

"Ain't it a horrible day?" they say. "It's raining."

But it ain't horrible to me. It makes me feel good.

I've even stopped saying to rain haters, "But I like rain." They think I'm fuckin' about. They look at me with a 'ha ha' expression on their face.

"Ol' Chas likes a laugh, don't he? How can he really mean he likes rain? How ridiculous!"

What shitbags they are.

Even the weathermen say it. "I'm afraid it's going to be a horrible day tomorrow. It's going to be raining."

They presume you're like them. More shitbag presumption. Why can't they just say, "It's going to be raining tomorrow," and leave it at that?

They're not there to give you their feelings. They're there to give you the weather forecast for fuck's sake. Before you know what, they'll start presuming you think like them in other things.

"It's going be a horrible day tomorrow. It's going to rain. So it'll be too wet to go to the beach. The one consolation being there'll be no chance of seeing the odd horrible fat bird in a bikini."

Now, I like fat birds in bikinis.

Well, not necessarily, but a lot of people do, and why not? The point I'm making is people presuming that if they don't like it, you don't like it. Prats.

Right, that's off my chest. They are fucking wankers though. Now calm down, Charlie boy.

BEETROOT

Beetroot grows on my allotment like a dream. It's a root vegetable, but unlike parsnip or carrot the root you eat (the variety I grow, Boltardy, a lovely ball) sits obligingly on top of the soil. So there's no problem with roots on my stony soil forking beneath the ground. The fine moisture-finding root beneath the ground gets cut off and don't get eaten anyway, so it can fork away to its heart's content if it wants – but, funny enough, in general it don't. Which proves to me that these root vegetables only do it when it matters - to annoy you.

Rabbits are partial to beetroot and will eat round a full-grown one, leaving it looking like a 'Beano Apple Core'. But they only usually munch on one or two and they haven't been too much of a nuisance in my experience. In fact on my allotment, and I've had it 10 years, I've had no trouble with them at all.

I do recommend the 'Boltardy' variety though. They really do have a resistance to 'bolting' or 'going to seed' before the root is fully developed.

Sow from April till July in rows 18 inches apart. Thin to 3 inches apart when the seedlings are an inch or so high, and then harvest every other one after they've reached golf ball size. July sowings won't mature fully but you'll get a good crop, well above golf ball size.

In fact, I just checked in my 2006 diary and I made a sowing on 22nd August. A note on 6th November says, "largest beetroot tennis ball size". So late season, about 10 weeks' worth of growth and well above golf ball size.

You can never gauge each season exactly like the last, but you're usually not far out. So it's well worth a late sowing.

Now think of peeling a vegetable - a potato, a parsnip, a swede. Not particularly an irksome task, but teetering on the tedious. Peeling a fresh-cooked beetroot, on the other hand, is quite the opposite. It's the loveliest thing.

Boil a good-sized beetroot for about 45 minutes and then run the pan under the cold tap to disperse the hot water. Grab hold of the beetroot and gently manipulate it between your fingers, getting the feel of it as though preparing to bowl a googly. The skin will fall away revealing a perfect, ready-to-eat, newborn vegetable - like a ripe-hot tit shedding a rough, raggedy brassiere.

You can pickle 'em if you want after cooking. It's not a bad idea. It's nice to have 'em at hand when you want 'em. Preferably use the first golf ball size pickings. Keep 'em in jars containing half vinegar, half water, in the fridge. Eat 'em with everything. Again, like red cabbage, they're lovely with egg and bacon.

The whole of the harvest can be eaten. Use the tops exactly like spinach. (Spinach beet is its relation.) In fact I think beetroot leaves have a better flavour than regular spinach. Jamie Oliver thinks so too.

When I was on Ready Steady Cook I took along my own beetroot and Brian Turner sliced the uncooked beetroot thin and fried it. Then he used the leaves as a salad garnish. It all turned out well tasty.

So beetroot for me is a 'must' crop on my allotment.

Just a word of warning though. Home-grown beetroot is so delicious that you will most likely eat it with everything. Just be aware that in the bathroom you'll piss pink and everything else will come out a deep shade of red.

Many a doctor's first question to a worried patient has been, "Have you been eating more than normal amounts of beetroot lately?"

But of course! I'm not bleeding to death internally after all! It was those five beetroots I ate with my bread and cheese last night!

Beetroot is completely pest free and every part of the plant can be eaten, so there's no waste.

I've found it happily stays in the ground until you want it throughout winter, but if in doubt (in case of an exceptionally severe winter) you can pull 'em late autumn and store 'em in sand in a barn or garage.

SWEETCORN

Now here's a good one to grow, although in England, not that many years ago, it wasn't.

My mum told me that my granddad tried growing it in the '40s, but just as it was coming to maturity down came the frosty, cold weather and 'out went the gas', as cousin Charlie, Spitfire pilot, used to say. Our season wasn't long enough. However, the gardening scientists worked on it and developed natural, tasty varieties that would mature in our short growing season.

I first grew sweetcorn in 1972 and, although I don't grow it every year, I almost do, as it's a good rock 'n' roll cropper. The reason I don't every year is because I like to give other things a go and I like the excitement of thinking after a couple of sweetcorn-free years, 'Okay, it's sweetcorn time again!' Then I usually go for it in a big way - half the plot; a forest of sweetcorn.

A full-grown sweetcorn plant is so impressive. You really feel you're at the top of your game when you've got a few of them on the go. And if you've got a hundred or more then it's akin to a 'to be reckoned with' plantation. They become sturdy 6-foot-plus trees from seed in the space of one summer.

The best way to start them off is in little Jiffy pots – small, individual, brown papier mâché looking pots. When ready, you plant the whole lot in the ground. This method of non-root disturbance really works. I've noticed that just after germination (the moment the seed begins to sprout) it grows a taproot many inches long while the green top growth is just reaching about an inch. Planting the whole thing don't disturb that root; it don't even know it has been transplanted and just merrily continues living life.

Disturbing or even breaking the root won't kill it. It just 'checks' the growth. This means it'll sit there not moving for a few days after transplanting thinking, 'Dunno what happened there. I think I had a blackout. What's happened to me feet? Fucking 'ell! I can't feel 'me feet!' Then it begins to find its feet again and off it goes. A few lost days.

But you don't lose any days with Jiffy pots, which can make a difference if it's a late sowing, which does happen.

Buy Jiffy pots about 1.5 or 2 inches in diameter. Sow two seeds in each pot and if they both germinate pull out the weakest.

Don't let 'em dry out. Keep 'em damp but not soggy. Let any newly sown seeds get too wet and they'll rot.

I plant 'em out when they've grown to about 3 or 4 inches, 15 inches apart in staggered rows. Plant 'em in blocks. That is, if for instance you plan for 25 plants, don't plant one row but rather 5 rows of 5. The pollen from the male flowers that grow at the top need to pollinate all the female cobs below, and so by planting out in a block they get more chance.

Harvesting
Don't make the mistake of letting the cobs fully mature before you snap 'em off for the cook pot (snap 'em off downwards) - the corn will look magnificent but they will now have turned to flour and no amount of cooking will tenderise them. They'll only be good for chicken feed.

So, the time to harvest?

The best advice I ever read was in an old American book.

Wait until the strands that grow out of the end of the cob begin looking like the tobacco in your granddads tobacco pouch. Then's the time to pick 'em: past the watery stage and into the milky, but before the starchy flour. Freeze any you can't use immediately. They freeze well.

I remember that tobacco in my granddads tobacco pouch. It smelt lovely. I liked the smell of him smoking it. But it didn't smell as good as it did in that tobacco pouch. Same as good coffee really. Coffee grounds smell better than the final brewed coffee for some reason and I don't know why. It still smells good but it don't smell as good as when you stick your nose in the tin.

So how many people now have granddads that roll their own or smoke a pipe? Well if you haven't you'll have to picture it: dried dark brown cob strands that can be smoked too. In this old American book the lady author would smoke it. I tried it and it was quite pleasant. I made a corn-cob pipe out of the corn I grew and puffed on it. It's probably less harmful than the regular stuff. I smoked a pipeful of culinary mixed herbs once. Don't do that. It done me head in rotten and had me believing I was a human banjo.

BEANS

Runner beans are absolutely the best, but they do have to be picked regular. At six to eight inches long, get 'em off the vine. Any longer and they will start to go stringy, and one stringy bean will spoil the whole fresh home-grown Sunday dinner runner bean treat.

So how does a rock 'n' roller cope with this one? Him who can't get down regular between piano solos to harvest the tender, unstringy beany boys?

I grow French climbing beans.

They're very nearly or probably just as tasty as the old-fashioned 'Scarlet Runner' while having the distinct advantage that they will spend quite a while longer on the vine before they start to go tough or stringy.

So I can now rock easy on the piano in those bean-harvesting weeks knowing that 'one more' on the piano don't mean 'one more' stringy bean.

The best way to start 'em off is again the old Jiffy pots, sweetcorn style. Put a couple of seeds in each pot and wait. If they both germinate, pull out the weakest.

When the plants are 3 or 4 inches high, plant the whole thing in the ground between sticks 6 inches apart. Set the sticks up (bamboo canes are the best) as follows. This is another old boy's tip, this time from Joan's Uncle Ben.

Buy 8-foot bamboo canes. Uncle Ben said these would be good for 5 years, and he was right. Push 'em into the soil at least 6 inches deep, leaving 6 inches between each and spacing the rows 18 inches apart. Make an X shape with them, but make the level at which they cross pretty low. This way, as Uncle Ben said, the majority of the beans will hang outwards, meaning they can be seen easily, like the old hop bines.

I tie all the canes along the row to each other. This creates a sturdy structure that's never let me down.

The Big Storm of 1987 lifted the roof off the chicken shed. I actually watched it float gracefully away over hedgerows and horsebean fields never to be seen again.

My mate Reggie Hawkins said his mate's chickens all got blew away to he knew not where in that same storm.

But my hop bine style French climbing bean structure never budged.

The dwarf varieties of the French bean ain't no slouches either. I grew some this year (2008). We're now in October and they're still having fun. And they well match the tastiness of the Scarlet Runner.

SWEARING

I originally decided not to swear in this book. I just wanted to see if I could do it. But as you may have noticed, I ain't found it easy. In fact I've just about abandoned the idea. I used quite a few swear words in my last book, Chas and Dave, All About Us, but it wouldn't have been authentic if I hadn't because a good part of it contained references as to what other people said. And other people swore a lot. Not excessively, really, but that was their own natural way of speaking.

Sentences were coloured with phrases like, "What a load of old bollocks" or "Don't be a cunt all your life" (take a day off), 'cos that's the way they spoke. Well, me too.

So it had to be done. Anything less wouldn't have been real.

I tried, but I've found it hard to write this book without my 'perfect punctuation' (that's what I call it) swear words.

And now I'm about to relate a story that involves 'piss' and I toyed with the idea of calling it urine. Actually I've got a feeling I've used 'piss' already, but it don't matter. Then I realised what a poxy word 'urine' is.

"He's urinated in his trousers." Sounds serious and terminal. He's in need of 24/7 nursing.

But "He's pissed hisself" just means 'give him a clean up and he's back up and running'.

Now what about this: "He caught his penis in his zip" or "He caught his knob in his zip". What sounds better?

It sounds like the 'penis' has no chance, but the 'knob' will definitely live to fight another day. The word 'knob' seems to have a bit of toughness about it.

'Penis in his zip' is a hospital job and a possible few days' stay, but 'knob in his zip' paints a picture of, "D'ya honestly think some trouser zip is gonna to get the better of my knob? I just zipped it back out again and went to the bar for another pint."

'Knob' is a much better word. It sits more comfortable … in your trousers, and in conversation.

'Penis' sounds like a wart you've got on your ear that you really must go and see the doctor about.

So folks, fuck it. It's been very, very hard curbing the lord mayoring but now, in a strange but joyful way, I feel liberated.

And so to the urine story …

I'll start here. It doesn't have to, but I want to. It will help to paint the picture and bring you in to the feel of the story.

On 27th December 1947, on the eve of my fourth birthday, my dad died. He shot himself. Nobody knew why. Two years later my mum married Larry Ferrar. She met him in the Exhibition pub where she played piano to earn money to feed us.

So Larry was now my stepfather. He was a tough guy. He was friends with (so he said) the bloke who banged the big gong at the beginning of the J. Arthur Rank films. He might've been. He was of the same stamp. But he never brought him round to tea.

Larry, in amongst all his toughness, was into growing flowers; sweet peas in particular. He worked at the Rolling Mills, Enfield, a big iron-smelting plant in its time.

He came home one day (as young as I was, aged five, I remember it) and he excitedly said to mum:

"I've been talking to a bloke at work who grows sweet peas. He reckons that the best way to water them is with piss. Keep 'em well watered and they'll thrive, he said, but water them with piss and they'll end up double the size!"

As we only had an outside toilet at the time, we all had pisspots. Therefore there'd be plenty of piss for Larry's flowers.

So Larry watered his beloved sweet peas from the family pisspots in the days that followed.

And did they thrive?

Did they fuck. They withered, turned black and died.

And Larry was none too pleased.

I know now that there is too much acid in newly produced piss. It's great for putting on the compost heap, as it speeds up the rotting down process nicely. When me and Dave were writing in my music shed down the end of the garden in the '70s our 'pissoir' was the compost heap, just outside the door. "That's where we piss of a night," Dave said in an interview. I've got a copy of it. Between us we produced good songs and good compost. That compost soon got rotted down and I grew great veg because of it. We downed a good quantity of Guinness in those days.

No, Larry wasn't a happy man. His beloved sweet peas, wiped out.

He went back to work next day gunning for the toerag so-called 'garden expert'.

I never found out the outcome. I'm guessing the garden adviser got wind and quickly found employment somewhere else.

You didn't fuck about with Larry.

Larry had an Alsatian dog when mum met him. Larry loved animals. That's mainly what attracted mum to him. Mum asked him where he'd got it.

"From a bloke who'd been mistreating it," said Larry.

"What? Did he abandon it?" asked mum.

"No," replied Larry, "I saw this bloke mistreating it in the street, so I went over to him, took hold of the lead and said, 'I'm having that dog, and you can fuck off."

Like I said, you didn't fuck about with Larry and, when it came to it, Larry didn't fuck about. Well, in that way anyway. He fucked about with stray crumpet and the marriage went wonky quick.

Mum's main loves, apart from music, were kids and animals. In general she didn't like grown-up people. She just loved animals and kids. And in her eyes they were the better judges of everything.

I remember giving my mum a bag of the first tomatoes I'd ever grown from seed. She was delighted. I rang her up the next day.

"Mum, what did you think of the tomatoes?"

"I tell you what, Chassie. You've grown a winner there! The parrot absolutely loved 'em!"

"But ...?!"

But no matter. It was genuine top praise from mum. She meant it.

CHICKENS

I do love chickens. But I'm not mad on ducks. They are just quacky, nervy things, but chickens, wherever they may be, just get on with it. Scratch away, two steps back, have a peck, scratch away, two steps back, have a peck. Sounds like a perfect dance to "Brazil, our hearts were generating June, we danced ...," etc. They just love life.

They can gang up on a cockerel though, if he's slow to show 'em who's boss.

I ain't saying nothing.

But, as I say, wherever they are, they just get on with it. That's what I like about chickens.

At the Spurs v. Man City Cup final in 1981 (I was there) somebody smuggled into the Wembley ground a real live cockerel. Now of course I ain't condoning this sort of thing, but the point I want to draw to your attention is the complete lack of concern the animal showed considering the ordeal it had just been put through after it got released onto the pitch during the pre-match kick about.

It just ruffled its wings back in shape with a casual 'fuck it, this don't look too bad' look on its face and off it went, the whole of Wembley pitch at his disposal. 'Scratch away, two steps back, have a peck, scratch away, two steps back ....' It wasn't phased at all. It wouldn't have mattered whether it was a gypsy camp or the gardens of Buckingham Palace. Live coverage on TV at Wembley? So what? Good grass. Good worms.

Footballers did headlong dives to try to catch him. Not a chance. He was too quick. Then, 'scratch away, two steps back, have a peck' ... 'Brazil, our hearts were generating June' ... 'Spurs are on their way to Wembley

…'!

I can't remember how they finally nailed him. I think they netted him. He was a star.

It was the most memorable event that day. Spurs only managed a boring draw, but they won the replay.

He probably ended up being part of the celebration dinner.

If you've got the ground it is well worth keeping chickens. Give 'em as much ground as you can, but make sure they can't get out to your vegetable patch. If they do they'll give it big stick and you'll rue the day you got 'em.

But keep 'em well penned and they are the food grower's best friend. Their manure is the best, containing four times as much nitrogen (for leaf growth) and phosphates (for root growth) as farmyard manure. Mixed with the straw I put in the chicken house it provides a humus-forming food for the soil. Use it as a top dressing and/or compost it.

All types of turds are good for the compost heap. My Uncle Will used to put tramp shit on his. Let me tell you a story he told me.

It wasn't actually his compost heap. Uncle Will employed it while helping out on a friend's farm during the war, doing general hedge cutting and farm tidying.

Any organic stuff would go on the compost heap, including the turds he began to find regularly on the ground in a gap in the hedge, the same gap almost every day. It was too big to be an animal's – well, not an animal you'd find running wild in Britain anyway. He'd shovel 'em up and compost 'em, but at the same time it was puzzling. So he decided to keep an extra eye out on that hedge.

The next morning he spotted Stinky, the village tramp, come wandering down the lane. He'd heard about him. As Stinky neared the gap in the hedge, down came his trousers, he done a shit, wiped his arse on a dock leaf and with a quick but satisfied glance round at the specimen, he hoisted up his trousers and was off down the road on his daily ponce.

The next day Uncle Will was ready for him.

No, he wasn't going to confront him, or bollock him, or anything like that. Uncle Will always looked towards the funny side of things and had a clever way of developing something funny into something even funnier.

Up his sleeve, he had a trick.

The next morning, at the same time, he spotted Stinky coming down the lane. Uncle Will crept along the other side of the hedge to the gap, keeping out of view of Stinky. They both got to the gap at the same time. Stinky pulled down his trousers on his side of the hedge and squatted. Uncle Will, on the other side of the hedge, slid a crafty shovel under Stinky's arse.

As Stinky reached for a dock leaf, unbeknown to him, Uncle Will quietly removed the shovel and turd. Then he stood out of sight to observe Stinky's reaction.

Arse wiped, trousers hitched, Stinky felt good. 'That come out well. Seemed like a long one, all in one piece.' That cod liver oil he'd been nicking from them riding school stables 'don't half do the trick'. Stinky looked round to view his latest production, but ...

Eh?! Where is it? Where the fuck's it gone? Perhaps it's rolled into a hole or something? No. Just plain, bare earth. No holes around. But there should be something. He had felt the movement of its journey into the outside world.

He pulls down his trousers and inspects 'em. Now this happened once before, a few months ago. A stray turd landed in the crutch of his trousers. But he felt it as soon as he pulled his trousers up. But this time? Not a sign of the whereabouts. No clue whatsoever. It's gone from the face of the Earth, just as though it never existed. Beam me up, Scotty! A happening wiped from history.

Deleted. Just like that.

Must be that home-made damson wine that Mrs Bartrop keeps giving me. Brain's getting addled. But that can't be right. Over-imbibing usually makes you forget things you've done. That ain't the case here. I'm remembering something that ain't been done! This is mad. Oh Christ! What the fuck's up?

After looking everywhere - in amongst the twigs of the hedge and even at one point, in sheer desperation, turning out his pockets - Stinky ambles off down the lane, just a little bit slower than his usual amble this time; a deep, thoughtful sort of amble.

Now let me think this out sensible. I'll lay the problem out in front of me. Now, it should have been there, directly below where my arse was, right bang underneath. Perhaps I should go back and check that dock leaf. That'll prove it ... No, fuck it, I'll just go back and do another one tomorrow and if the same thing happens I'll give up Mrs Bartrop's damson wine. Or go down the doctors. Or both. Whatever, I'll certainly give it a major crap scan. I think I'll get an early night tonight.

It reminded him of the joke where the bloke had shit on a tortoise. But in the joke the bloke sat and pondered for a while, giving the tortoise enough time to wander off. Stinky's one was a quick one. No tortoise could've been that fast.

So the next day Stinky wanders down Turd Lane till he finds the gap in the hedge. Uncle Will spots him, but this time he lets Stinky be.

Trousers down, job done, arse wiped, Stinky hoists his trousers up.

But his face was the picture of a troubled man. He was scared stiff of looking round.

Then courage came. Chin up, chest out, he knew what had to be done.

He turned to look.

And ... bugger me! There it was!

Hallelujah! Shout out loud. It's brown and I'm proud! I'm back in the land of the living!

His face shone with happiness and he skipped down the lane with the feeling that all was well with the world once again.

Now I've wandered from the plot one more time.

But there was a common denominator. Now what was it? ... Got it!

Turds.

Chickens turds, then Stinky's. So back to chickens.

Feed 'em Layers Mash and let 'em have all the scraps and green stuff you can - cabbage leaves, spinach, or whatever will guarantee that your eggs will sit proud in the pan with a healthy-looking orange tinge. And you won't find any as good in the shops, no matter what any advert says.

A secure pen has a twofold purpose: to stop the chickens getting out and to prevent a fox from getting in. But as long as you bolt the door after the chickens have returned to their house at dusk you shouldn't have a problem. There are many stories about how crafty the fox can be, and he sure can be, but I've never heard of a fox undoing a door bolt.

Chickens attract rats because they like the food and if left unchecked you'll soon be overrun with 'em. When I first saw one I thought, 'Oh he ain't doing much harm. One little rat. He can't help being a rat. It ain't his fault. I'll leave him. He won't eat a lot.' Big mistake. But pretty soon he'd had a family. Seven rats! Then they all have families. Seven sevens are 49, seven forty nines are 343. In no time at all you've got 343 rats. So don't feel sentimental about the first one you see. Do away with him as soon as possible. He's only one. If you don't you'll soon have 343 that will have to suffer, and if you don't get them, they'll soon be seven times that, 2,401. And then they'll get you. So kill the first one and think

Spring is near!

Runner bean trench
(filled with manure)

Could be an allotment
on Glastonbury!

A birds eye view of a tomato plant

My granddaughter Charlie,
daughter Juliet and wife Joan

My Allotment in 2001.
Onions, spinach, carrots and
young sweetcorn (top right)

Top: Me with my
granddaughter Charlie
at the allotment in 2001

Right: Summertime!

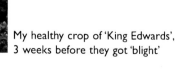

My healthy crop of 'King Edwards',
3 weeks before they got 'blight'

Idyllic! Joan is doing me a cup of tea while I'm about to thin out those onions. That's my old 1943 willys jeep on the left

Above: In the garden behind the runner beans. The family in the background. 1975.

Left: Helping hands!

Above: This is the best way to set your runner bean sticks.

Left: Proud grower!
(of beard and lettuce!), 1990.

Left: Me and Charlie

Below: Grown in my old garden where 'blight' was never a problem!

Panda's pickles

Above: It'll all look different come spring!

Left: Heading home for tea!

how many rats lives you're saving!

I was sitting by the garden pond one day in late autumn when the chickens were out. It was the end of the season on a nice sunny afternoon. There was nothing left in the garden that I objected to the chickens pecking at, so they were allowed to run free. They were merrily pecking their food from a dish by their shed and a robin joined in. I was marvelling at how they all mucked in together, no bother. Then, like a flash, a rat shot from under the shed, grabbed the robin, and dragged him back under the shed. The squeaking was horrible. The gap under the shed was only around two inches. I was helpless.

So I vowed to get that little shitbag ... and his mates.

I thought, okay, I've got an air rifle. I'll lay some bait close to where he runs in and out under the shed and lie in wait. I did. I was hiding by the apple tree. Out he came. Ping. Missed! He's back underneath the shed with the bait.

Now rats are very, very clever. That's why they are still around, though for hundreds and hundreds of years man has tried to exterminate them to extinction. And that is exactly why they are clever. Over all those years the dumb ones get caught, leaving the clever ones to reproduce. So with each generation they get cleverer and cleverer. You can trick a rat once, but it don't fall for the same trick twice. I've had first-hand experience a few times.

Just as I write this we are in the process of getting rid of a rat, or some rats, in our backyard. We've had the rat man round. He's great. He thinks like a rat. He looks like a rat. But a young, lively, clever, smart, top-of-the-tree rat that knows what rats get up to only too well. He obviously used to be one. He don't take no nonsense. He'll tell you to check traps regularly. Rats shouldn't suffer. I agree.

The rats have found entry into the roof of the house

through the roof of the kitchen. So between me and the rat man we found the entry hole. He gave me a trap to set. I baited it with chocolate, snapping a small piece off and putting it in the middle of the set-up trap. The next day the chocolate was gone, but the trap stayed set.

So (this was only last week) I began to think clever - like a rat. Instead of snapping off a piece of chocolate and placing it in the middle of the trap, I decided to melt some chocolate and pour it into the middle of the trap. That way it couldn't be nicked. It would have to be gnawed at.

Well, it done the trick. I heard the snap of the trap while I was writing here a couple of days ago at about 2 o'clock in the morning. I checked straight away. It was well clean, straight across the neck. Didn't know a thing about it.

Now I know there's at least one rat left. I can't hear them or it in the roof anymore, but the reset trap has twice been ejected from the hole and into the yard. Spooky. Both times the trap snapped, but no rat.

At this moment, it is now set, melted chocolate, ready to go, in the roof rat entrance. I'll keep you posted.

(Three weeks later: the trap's still baited up with chocolate but they're steering clear. They're clever. Rat man's coming round Monday. He'll figure out something.)

But back to 1976 and the stalking of the rat who killed poor Cock Robin.

One go with my air rifle from behind the apple tree. Missed.

This needs some rat-like thinking. The next day at dusk I baited up again, but this time thinking rat-like clever. That's the way.

I placed the bait three inches from his front door. I didn't hide behind the apple tree. Instead I lay full length on top of the shed with my rifle pointing straight down about two inches above the bait and an inch from his front door, reckoning on it being positioned right above his head when he came out sniffing. I was right! After about ten minutes, out came his nose … then his head. The rifle snout was now right above his and - ping! Bingo! Instantly brown bread.

Now for his mates. I managed to trick two of 'em into it! These must've been some dumb rats. But then the rest twigged and disappeared to I know not where. They do this.

I showed the dead rats to Dave. He was impressed with my marksmanship - straight between the eyes. Good shot, eh? I wallowed in it for a while (well, a few seconds), then I told him how I done it.

And the birds of the air quit a-sighing and a-sobbing, when they heard I shot the rat who killed poor Cock Robin. And I shot the Deputy … and his mate.

One more rat story, this time Uncle Alf's.

It was in the '30s and he told me you could buy this super sticky glue that never set. You daubed it all round a board, leaving a space in the middle, and in that space you put some rat bait. The idea was that the rat would crawl on the board after the bait and get stuck, to be disposed of by you.

So Uncle Alf set out the board one day. On checking after dark, he found no takers. He didn't think much more of it. Sort it out tomorrow. Another useless rat-catching gimmick. Went to bed.

The next morning he went out to dispose of the rat-catching gimmick and there, on the board, were two rats' feet. A rat had got caught and had gnawed off its own feet to get away.

I know, it's horrible! But I'm only telling you what Uncle Alf told me!

Anyway, back to chickens …

Me and Joan first decided to get chickens in 1973, just after me and Dave got together.

We decided on ten chickens and bought them from

Mr Ken Newlands, who had a poultry farm in Henham … close to a village called Chickney.

No, they're nowhere near Trumpton or Camberwick Green, they're just outside Stanstead Mountfitchet, not far from Ugley and Maggots End. (Put it in your sat-nav if you don't believe me!)

Mr Newlands' poultry farm was unique.

We bought POL (point of lay) hens (ones that were just a few weeks old). But he had all manner of poultry on his well rambling farm.

On first sighting the place, you could be forgiven for thinking you had happened upon an old vehicle dumping ground. But on closer inspection of that old '60s mini-van, there'd be a peacock perching on the steering wheel merrily squirting shit all over the dashboard and his wife and kids pecking corn and water out of the ashtrays. The windows were wound down just enough for air, but not enough to get through. A perfect temporary home, in fact.

Next to it would be a late '40s Ford Shooting Brake, worth potentially hundreds of pounds (thousands now). In it would be a bundle of happy baby pheasants, cheerfully perching and depositing tiny pheasant turds all over the once plush leather seats. They would give you a look of both wonder and contentment as you gazed in on 'em, as if to say, "What a lovely home we've got. Don't you wish you could live here too?"

They say that people often resemble the animals that they love. Mr Newlands fitted that theory. He loved poultry. He always wore a crisp brown overall with loads of pens in the top pocket and had the appearance and movements of a smart bantam cock. I don't know if I imagined it or not, but I'm sure his neck did a slight back and forwards 'one, two' cockerel-like jerk as he walked. Whatever, he was well 'poultrified'.

He was a member of the local amateur dramatics society. We planned to go to see him in one of his productions, but it never came about. He came to see us though, me and Dave. Him and his pal and I think their two lady friends came to see us in Bishop Stortford.

When me and Joan next saw him I asked him if he'd enjoyed it.

He hadn't.

"I didn't like the song about the pair of testicles," he said.

In those days we used to do 'The Bollocks Song'(must revive it) and invite the punters to sing along, "You can call 'em testicles or knackers or cobblers, nuts or balls, but 'BOLLOCKS!' (and everyone shouts it out) says it all!"

No, Mr Newlands weren't none too pleased with this one but we still stayed friends.

We always got our Christmas turkey from him. Early Christmas Eve we'd turn up at his farm. Out he'd come, covered from head to foot in white turkey feathers. The whole week he'd been plucking turkeys, from morning till night. He'd come out and tell us about it. He sort of moaned but seemed excited about it at the same time. It was the closest he came to being actual poultry himself, covered in all those white feathers. It was a happy time for him really, and of course for us.

He told me once that there was a cockerel you could get that was turkey size. Not massive, but at least twice the size of a chicken and fattened up in the proper way. Now I fancied this idea instead of a turkey one year, just for a change. So did Joan when I suggested it to her. Turkey meat can be dry sometimes but usually chicken ain't.

"Get me one!" I said. "We wanna give it a go!"

But he never did. He came forth with every other request but not this one.

I reckon it was a personal thing. He, the smart bantam cock, though admitting that these fat birds did actually exist, reckoned they were neither fish nor fowl nor anything. They were there to be talked about, but to have no truck with. His delivery of information about these birds was devoid of any emotion either way, but I suspect he told me about these outsize cockerels expecting a 'whatever next?' response.

His POL hens were top class and he knew how to catch 'em. You've gotta be quick, I learnt, but stealthy at the same time. They move fast.

I'd say, for instance, that I wanted six and into the pen he'd go. Fifty hens would run away from him into the furthest corner. Then he'd crouch and move in a slow, prowling way towards them. They'd eye him up. Then he'd position an outstretched palm over one of the hens, about two feet above it, moving his palm slowly downwards. The bird wouldn't run, but would crouch down while the rest scooted. Then - wallop! Out would go the hand and a leg would be grabbed. Squawking would ensue, but once held upside down calmness would prevail. One down, five to go.

I asked him why the bird he held his hand over didn't run like the rest of them. He was a polite man.

"It's a bit embarrassing explaining this in front of your wife." he said.

"I don't really see?" I responded. What on earth could it be?

"I'd like to know!" insisted Joan.

"Well," he said, "when she sees my hand hover over her, her senses say it's a cockerel and she is about to be mated, so she squats down, ready."

No wonder she squawks when, instead of getting 'that', a leg is grabbed and she's instantly hoisted upside down. That ain't no way to treat a lady.

But I do remember Joan saying once when we got our first batch of hens and a cockerel, "I don't think the hens enjoy being mated very much. He's just on her like a flash, grabs the back of her neck with his beak and – bosh - it's all over and done with."

I think she thought that when they got the urge the cock and hen would find a nice, soft bit of hay and after a bit of cuddling and snogging the hen would succumb. She'd lie back and open her legs and the cockerel would be at it for a half-hour or so. Then he'd have a fag afterwards, while the hen had a bath.

A lovely dust bath!

They do love a dust bath, especially in the ash dust from the fire grate. I used to put it straight into their run. They liked the warmth of the 'next day' ashes. They would run headlong and jump in. Sometimes, though, it would still be a bit on the hot side, ashes having not cooled down enough. They'd jump straight out with a look of: holy shit! That's too fuckin' hot!

But, not to be beat, they'd circle the pile of ashes like Red Indians, but in slow motion, round a wagon train circle, testing the ash temperature every now and then.

Then, when it was just right, like baby bear's porridge, in they'd go again. Wings and bodies going wild. Happiness and ash dust filling the air.

DUCKS, MORE CHICKENS AND THE TWO OL' GELS NEXT DOOR

We kept Aylesbury ducks for a while at one time. Well, a duck and a drake.

They've got a different way of mating to chickens. Actually, on second thoughts, there are similarities. They've got the same 'beak and bosh' method. But he liked to get her when she was swimming on our little garden pond, just after she'd preened herself.

In she'd go, stretching and flapping her wings on the water before settling down sedately to a serene and gentle paddle. Then in he'd go. 'Now is that a sexy bird or what? Get in there my son!' Straight in the deep end, on her back, head held down in the water with his beak and – bosh! - job done. Then back on the bank, on the cadge for snout (Cockney for fag/cigarette).

Joan's brother, Bruce, has got a river outside his door. Not long ago he said, "The other day I saw a duck bullying another duck. It jumped on its back and was trying to drown it by holding its head down with its beak."

Before I got a chance to say anything he continued, "I chucked a brick at it. It only just glanced off it, but it put a stop to his little lark!"

"Bruce! His little lark was him giving her one!"

He'd probably been eying up that duck for weeks. Her playing hard to get, but making sure he was watching, flapping her wings and preening. And so, a little swim, pretending to be oblivious of his ogling.

'Now's me chance!' he's thought. 'I'm having some of

that!' Wallop! In he's gone. But then a 'wallop' he wasn't expecting - a brick at the side of the head.

'This is some bird!' he dazedly thought. 'She packs some punch!' But end of romance I would say.

'I like a drake to give me good 'beak and bosh'. Got 'beak' alright, but 'bosh' was a washout.'

He won't get no second chance. All Bruce's fault.

Ducks seem to be pretty poor mothers. Well, Aylesbury ducks are anyway. Or at least our one was. The hens took all the babies on. As well as being hatched by 'em, they'd all snuggle under the hens' wings. The hen would manage to find room for the lot - baby ducks and baby chickens and all. It's a lovely sight to see. Some might think, 'What's the use of wings on a hen? She can't fly.' But watch her swaddle her chicks and others' chicks with 'em and you'll go, 'Now that's what they're for! That is happiness! For the chicks and mum.'

Chickens know when it's time for bed. As the day draws to a close they will wander one by one towards their house, hop in, and so to perch. That school song goes through my head as I watch 'em. 'Now the day is over, night is drawing nigh.'

When you get a new batch of chickens they soon settle in and get to know where their house is. When they do, they don't forget.

One year I moved their house to a different patch, just 25 feet away from where it used to be, to rest the ground. They were in and out of it and pecking around it all day, but at nightfall they all entered the Twilight Zone.

One by one they all gathered at the entrance of where the house used to be. They just stood there in a bunch, heads in the direction of the missing house. Then they looked round at each other with some 'anybody got any ideas?' neck jerking. Then some positive, 'some cunt's had our house away,' indignant clucking noises.

I gently herded them towards its new location. After a

couple of days the chickens' pennies dropped.

Unlike chickens, ducks don't head for home at night. They just squat down where they are. You have to put 'em in. If you don't, Mr Fox is soon sniffing round. I know this only too well.

One night, Joan was up the hospital visiting her dad, and I was supposed to put Dandy the duck in the chicken house at dusk. I forgot. I scooted up the yard an hour after dark expecting to see him huddled up in the middle of the yard. He wasn't. No Dandy duck. Just white feathers everywhere. Mr Fox had got there first.

Joan was upset, to say the least. The next morning she went straight to Mr Newlands' poultry farm and bought another duck, a baby Aylesbury. She named him Dandy in memory of the departed.

He couldn't go on the garden pond yet because he was too young and his feathers hadn't got their 'oils'. He would sink if he did. So we kept him penned in by the house for a few weeks until his feathers were ready.

I made a nice little enclosure, he was kept fed and watered, and he was very happy. When the time is right, we can let him out.

In the meantime, the two old sisters next door, Glad and Grace, had begun acting offish towards us. An ominous sign of a new moan on the horizon. That was nothing unusual. There was always something: the usual football over the garden fence; nailing Catherine Wheels to their fence posts; using their fence for our runner beans to climb up.

But this time it was more mysterious. Every time they came into their garden, they made a point of looking over the fence and scowling down towards where the new Dandy duck was penned in by the house.

But still they were saying nothing. We were puzzled. Just what was it this time?

Finally, after a couple of days, Grace, who was the older and more deaf of the two said to Joan over the fence, "It's no good. I can't bottle it up any longer. I've got to speak to you about the way you're treating that duck!"

"What do you mean, Grace?" said Joan.

It had a nice little enclosure, plenty of food and water. The little duck was as happy as a sandboy. It almost smiled when it looked at you.

"The way you're starving it and keeping it away from that pond!" she replied.

Starving it? It's got plenty of food. But the pond bit? Don't she know? She kept ducks and chickens in her younger day.

"He can't go on the pond till he GETS HIS 'OILS'!" Joan shouted down her ear. "And what do you mean, starving it? He's got PLENTY OF FOOD!"

But she ain't heard.

"That duck," she said, "used to be big and healthy. We used to love watching it on the pond. Look at it now! Poor thing. Wasting away! You should be thoroughly ashamed of yourselves!"

Joan finally, incredulously, got her gist. She thinks it's the original Dandy duck!

This one's something like half the size from its head to its tail! No matter how anything gets starved, it can only get thinner. It don't get shorter!

Imagine it. Going on a crash diet to look more attractive to the ladies and after a couple of months you're a foot shorter. Great! That'll do it. That'll get all the crumpet running after me.

But …

"Grace! IT'S NOT THE SAME DUCK!"

"We know youngsters today are different to our day, but we thought you were a bit different. It seems that we were wrong. Treating an animal like that!"

"GRACE!" Joan said slowly and as stentorian as she could, "IT'S NOT THE SAME DUCK!"

In the meantime Gladys had stridden into the garden

to have her say, and she caught Joan's last sentence. Her hearing was better than Grace's. The look on her face said she'd got the message even before Joan spoke.

"Glad!" said Joan, "Can you tell Grace that this little duck we have now has not been starved down. It is not the original duck. Sadly that duck was got by the fox and I bought this baby one the next day. It's penned in because it can't go on the pond yet. As soon as it can, it will, and will be flapping its wings in the water and enjoying itself just like the old one did. Only this time he'll be housed up every nightfall."

"Grace," said Glad, "It's not the same duck."

Grace immediately understood and waddled down the garden path back to the house.

How comes she couldn't be got through to by Joan as easy?

But Glad and Grace were sisters.

Old Mr Newlands taught me a lot about poultry. I had to grab the chickens one by one and puff powder all over 'em one year to de-flea 'em. I would never have caught 'em if I hadn't watched him. I found out they had fleas by accident.

I'd come in from a gig one night, had a beer, and before going to bed thought I'd creep down to the end of the garden to see how they were. I hadn't long made a new hut for 'em. I'd put in a perch, but had noticed about a week before that it was full up with chickens and there was one left squatting on the floor. My chicken book said how they love to perch, so the day before I managed to fit another perch beneath the existing one for the other hen. Great! Now all are comfortable.

So off I've gone, down to the end of the garden. I opened up the back of the hen house and shone my torch in. There, sat on the top perch, was a row full of hens. And there, sat on the perch directly below, was the lone hen - covered in shit. It had come from those perched directly above. It was my fault. She looked round at me and if she could've spoken there was only one word she would've called me.

I slung my head in the back of the hut and removed the perch there and then, giving the hen a comfortable straw-filled corner for the night while rethinking the perch position for the morrow.

Back indoors, I was about to head for bed, but annoyingly my head suddenly began to itch. Now I washed my hair before going out tonight. So it ain't in need of that. So why's it doing this? I continued with the head scratching. (I bet you're scratching now. Power of suggestion. I know I am.) There on my hand appeared a couple of tiny red crawly things. What's this all about? Are there more in my hair? One way to find out. I held my head over the white enamel surface we had in the kitchen and ruffled my hair. Hundreds dropped out. I was lousy with these fucking little chicken flea things.

I discovered the next day that the inside of the chicken house was running alive with these tiny little shitbags.

I hosed the whole house out and limewashed it (a mixture of lime and water). Then I dusted the chickens one by one with special flea powder, catching 'em Mr Newlands style. 'Whole Lotta Squawking Goin' On' – but, given sense, them chickens would've thanked me.

About a mile down the road from where we lived in Broxbourne was St Giles hall, Nazeing, to be visited on jumble sale occasions and the twice yearly flower and vegetable show.

I liked the autumn flower and vegetable show best. It's a nice time of year. 'All is safely gathered in, ere the winter storms begin' - a good 'Harvest Home' song. I've got pleasant memories of singing it in the school hall while the stage was adorned with impressive, cleverly plaited, baked loaves in the shape of sheaths of corn, the words on the top saying, 'Happy Harvest' and 'Our Daily Bread'. Wonderful bakery.

We were asked to bring food for the old people.

Tinned food would be fine. This didn't seem right to me - in amongst the biblical stuff, Jesus with a tin opener. My mate's donation of a tin of pilchards sitting among those magnificent loaves bore out my reckoning. But then I suppose, once on a dish, the loaves and fishes in a church situation do only conjure up one person – Jesus - tin opener or not. But of course, with a tin of pilchards, he would need to be 'more tin opener' than 'not' … unless he had a Swiss army knife.

You can actually open a tin of pilchards with a Swiss army knife. I've done it. It takes about a whole morning but it can be done, and what better way to spend a morning if you happen to be out of bed? (My mornings don't begin the day. They end with bedtime at 4 a.m. and I begin the day at noon. What a wonderful life!)

Pilchards need a tin opener because they don't have that handy little key attached to the tin like sardines do (well they did when I last looked). The key that, on opening the tin, ended up being attached to that lethal (if you're not careful) coil of metal that your granddad chucked in the dustbin along with the key. The same one that you fished out, unwinding the coil of metal, cutting yourself several times (no, you were not careful) to get the key with the slot in that was too good to throw away. Can this be used with something clockwork that you've got? Of course. Big possibility. Must make it to be. But look, just get it and sort that out later. The dustbin is meant for tins, fish bones, potato peelings and ash from the fire grate, not for metal keys with smart slots in. Not while I'm around. They ain't rubbish looking material. Too slinky and out there on their own. I'll find a use for them.

I can't remember how they got there, but I've got a couple in my toolbox now. It's never too late.

Sometimes in the '70s Broxbourne years, in the 'all was safely gathered in' seasons, I'd enter vegetables I thought suitable in the flower and vegetable show.

However, I quickly found out that this vegetable show caper was a whole new ball game. It was nothing to do with growing food. Taste never entered into it. For instance, if you were entering parsnips, the complete taproot had to be intact down to the very end. This was most important. So you would have to dig down about a yard (metre), carefully watering all the time, to be able to get the whole thing out. It would end up being about a yard long, from about three inches or so diameter at the top down to nothing at the bottom.

So you entered a yard-long parsnip, whereas in the kitchen you'd only use the first nine or ten inches. The 'rat's tail' of the rest is of no use. But it was to the judges. In addition, your entries had to be almost identical in size. I think it was three or five of each variety you had to enter. I saw the entries but I never entered in the parsnip class.

But I did enter with carrots and onions one year. The carrots came second but the onions, although they were the biggest in the show, only got a 'commended' certificate. These were my 'Robinson's Mammoth' onions. (After a few years' gap I'm growing these again this year. Well tubby and tasty.) Two of them were the size of bowling green balls and three were the size of reasonable coconuts. I was told nicely that they would've won if the whole five had been of similar size. So I wasn't going to get into that. I was into growing organic vegetables for the purpose of feeding the family. Competitions were fun and not to be taken serious in my mind.

But I was about to get a shock from the old gels next door.

The straight-laced churchgoers lived their lives by the book and were quick to poke their noses into yours, bringing to your attention their book rules as and when they thought fit, which was a good part of the time.

The first time I remember there being a hosepipe ban,

I decided to use it regularly, but sparsely, only to fill up the chickens' water, which was down at the end of the garden. Yes, I was using the banned hosepipe, but I wasn't using any more water than I would've done anyway. It just meant that I didn't have to carry water in a can 70-odd yards from kitchen to coop every day. But to them I was committing a heinous crime.

"You know you're not supposed to use the hosepipe! We're not using ours!" And so on.

So what a surprise on discovering the purpose of an enquiry one sunny late summer afternoon.

"Have you got any beetroot growing?" said Gladys over the fence.

I did. Whatever you alternate over the years, beetroot has to be grown, as well as onions, every year - so trouble free and so well above any shop quality.

"Yes I have. Why? Do you want some?"

"Well, I only want one. I've got plenty growing, but I need just one."

What did she mean?

"You're welcome," I said. "But I don't get it. Why do you need one if you've got plenty?"

"Well it's the show. You've got to have five of uniform size to be in with a chance of winning and I've only got four. I thought you might have one of the same size I could have."

I don't believe what I'm hearing! These churchgoing, straight-laced old ladies up for fraudulent practice dabbling?

"I can't do that, Gladys. That's out-and-out cheating!"

"Mr Boxhall does it. They all do it. Mr Turner's bought them from the shops."

I can't believe it. All these 'you youngsters of today' old people on the cheat. Surely old people never used to be like this years ago?

I didn't give in. I thought these oldsters have got to learn the hard way. I must be firm and stand by all those adages. 'I'll be making a rod for my own back.' 'Give 'em an inch and they'll take a mile.' 'Got to be cruel to be kind.'

They sulked a bit but they never asked again. You do feel you're being a bit harsh, but you've got to say to yourself that you're doing it for their own good.

One day, they'll look back and say, "Thank you, children. We were straying from the path of righteousness. But you, in your young wisdom, put us back on track. We wouldn't be the old people we are today if it weren't for you."

POTATOES AND TOMATOES

I haven't grown potatoes lately on my allotment, mainly 'cos my rock 'n' roll lifestyle requires the least troublesome crops. So why are they troublesome for me? Read on.

I've had this particular plot for some 10 years now, and more often than not, just when the crop is thriving, around deep summer, down comes blight.

On my and our whole allotment it's a particular nuisance. It's almost as though it comes in through the gate. Vito gets it first. His plots are just inside the gate. Then we know we're all in for it. It creeps its way along all our plots, leaving no tater unblighted.

It loves warm, wet, muggy weather. It's a fungus that gets washed down into the soil. The leaves turn black and soon the whole crop goes rotten. Tomatoes get trounced too, being of the same family.

In 2002 (just checked the diary) blight came around on 13th August and my healthy crop of King Edwards (see picture) was wiped out virtually overnight. It's like the plague. You can imagine potatoes being taken away in little coffins as you paint a red cross on the allotment shed door. 'Bring out your dead.' Whole families of 'em. It's so sad.

There are precautions you can take like spraying with Bordeaux Mixture for instance. I'm not sure if this is organic or not, but you can check it out in another gardening book. I don't know if it works either, 'cos I've not tried it.

On my original plot at old Nazeing Road when the kids were young I had no such trouble with potatoes. Blight was non-existent in the 10 years I cultivated that plot. So what did I learn about growing potatoes in those 10 blightless potato-growing years that might be beneficial to you?

1. It's only worth growing potatoes if you've got the space. Don't try to save space by planting them close together, which I've done in the past. You'll think you're doing alright because the top growth will flourish and look healthy, but it's only just fighting for the light. It won't have a lot of strength left to make reasonable potatoes in the ground. When you dig 'em up there won't be a lot; if any, sometimes.

2. Just grow 'early' potatoes ('new' potatoes), planted around the end of March or early April. They're a good rock 'n' roll cropper mainly because they don't get bothered much by slugs like 'lates' do. But that ain't all. 'Early' or 'new' potatoes taste the best, as you might well know. So they're well worth growing.

What about second 'earlies' and maincrop ('lates')? Well, that's up to you. In my experience that's when the slugs and the blight (on my allotment) move in, so not a rock 'n' roll crop for me as they need more looking after.

So how do you grow 'em? There are tips that will give you a maximum crop that are worth exploring in other books later on. Of course you can swot up right away if you want, but these tater tips that follow will get you on the way and buzzing for the home-grown spud.

All gardening books are worth a read. The answers that you're looking for you may not find in one book, but you'll find them in another. Often you'll read something and go, 'That's a good idea,' and give that a go.

But here's my starter for potatoes. It's a simple method that'll get you going and will give you a reasonable crop. You can start to fine-tune it next time around.

Buy your 'new' seed potatoes from a garden centre in January. You won't need to plant 'em until the end of

March but don't wait till then to buy 'em as they'll all be gone. Growing your own is getting more and more popular all the time.

Straight away they need frost-free light and air. This is what I do (my wife quite likes the effect). I place them close together in between ornaments and knick-knacks on the sill of our south-facing bay window. South-facing windows get maximum sunlight.

So all the spaces between the ornaments are now taken up with seed potatoes, sprouts facing upwards. The potatoes will develop nice little tough green sprouts and will be well ready to go forth and multiply when you plant them at the end of March.

With a trowel, plant the new potatoes 4 inches deep, sprouts uppermost, 12 inches apart in rows 18 inches apart. As soon as the shoots begin to show, use a swan-necked hoe to cover them with earth ('earthing up'). Continue to do this as they poke through until you can't do it anymore. This will protect against late frost while healthy growth will flourish beneath the soil.

Wait until the tops start to die down before you are tempted to dig a root. And then, dig your fork deep, but a good foot away from the top growth to avoid spearing the Sunday dinner specials.

You've got less chance of being bothered by blight or slugs with early potatoes. It's only the later maincrop that the slugs seem to home in on.

Actually, when my big maincrop King Edwards copped blight, I got out all my gardening books and read up and then combined the advice.

1. Cut all the tops off, leaving just short stalks. What infect the potato are fungus spores on the leaves that get continually washed into the soil, so doing this will help.

2. Only dig the potatoes as needed. Don't dig and store. Apparently they will infect each other.

I ended up not doing too badly in fact. The potatoes hadn't had time to grow to full maturity but they were at least around cricket ball size. Out of the whole crop I think I only had one soggy blighted one, so not bad at all.

But yes, it did put me off growing them again in large quantities. I had plans for a massive store of King Edwards to last the year round and it didn't happen.

I had also stopped growing tomatoes on my allotment - not worth the blight risk. But it was such a shame 'cos I love 'em, especially the home-sown/-grown ones.

So I decided to give 'em another go in 2006.

I was recording in Lyles, Tennessee in 2005, at my pal J.I. Allison's ranch. (He wrote songs like, 'That'll Be the Day', 'Peggy Sue' and 'Think It Over' with Buddy Holly.) It was just me and him. We'd known each other for years and had kept saying we would, and finally we were recording some rock 'n' roll together.

As well as being impressed with his rock 'n' roll drumming, as usual, I discovered that he also grew nice tomatoes. The variety was called 'Bradley'.

After dinner one night at his house, I asked his wife Joanie for a piece of kitchen towel. On it I spread out some seeds I'd saved from a Bradley tomato, left it on her window sill for a couple of days to dry and took them back home to England.

Back home, when we got to the month of April, I separated the seeds by removing them carefully from the kitchen towel with a pair of tweezers. They only needed to be roughly separated. Bits of towel sticking to them don't matter.

Then I filled 12 3-inch flowerpots with seedling compost (you can buy this) and sowed three seeds on the surface, or no deeper than the depth of the seed, and set the little pots out on a south-facing window sill.

I then waited for the 'seed leaves' ('cotyledon leaves') to burst through. These are the first two leaves to appear and are a different shape to all the leaves that follow. At point I thinned them down to the one that was the strongest in each pot and left it to grow on.

I kept 'em in pots on a south-facing window sill until the end of May and then planted them out in the open, 2 feet apart each way.

You can still get a late frost but you're usually okay from June onwards. I staked and 'pinched out' (look in another book!) every plant and was looking forward to these Tennessee tomatoes.

I had 12 sturdy plants and the tomatoes began to ripen nicely. They looked so good. I've gotta be in luck this time, I thought.

But no! Just as we were coming into August, that old enemy blight reared its ugly head again.

Overnight they keeled over, turned black and rotted away. It put me off growing them again, at least on the allotment.

It's a shame, but there you are. On my old Broxbourne plot I grew tomatoes over ten summers with not a sign of blight. On my allotment in the ten years I've had it, only a couple of years have been blight-free.

I do so love to grow tomatoes from seed. You have a far bigger choice than just seeing what plants they've got in the garden centre. Also you can save seeds from a tasty tomato like I did. I love doing things like this. They don't always grow true to the fruit you got it from, but that's all part of the fun of gardening. But it's such a git when you've brought 'em up from seed and then just when they're about to ripen along comes the Black Blight.

So the 'Bradley' Tennessee tomatoes never came to fruition, but the 'Chas and J.I.' album did. It came out in 2007 on Sanctuary Records and was called 'Before I Grow Too Old'. We had great fun doing it and were pleased with the result.

Having said all that, I've got some tomato plants on my allotment at this very moment (July 2008) that my

Italian mate Vito (down the end of the allotment) gave me. He'd done all the hard work growing 'em from seed, so all I had to do was plant 'em, and it was worth another go.

Only this time I've decided I'm not going to the trouble of tying them to bamboo canes and pinching out the side shoots. I'm gonna get a bail of straw tomorrow, spread it thick around the plants and let 'em grow as 'bush' tomatoes, just let 'em go wild. The straw will act as a 'mulch' and will keep the tomatoes off the earth. There are about 24 plants and you can bet your life if I spend time staking and pinching out, just when I'm done and am standing back proud, blight will strike again. And in come the little tomato coffins.

Update...

So how did they fare? Well, it's now two months later, September 2008, so here we go.

My daughter Kate, who loves my allotment produce, as do baby Harry and husband Paul, rang me last month while I was on the road. It wasn't good news: "I'm over the allotment, dad. Everything looks lovely except the tomatoes."

Now I'd only seen 'em two days before and they were strong, sturdy bushes. But I know how quick blight strikes.

My fears were confirmed when I got down there a couple of days later. The tomato patch was a black mass of dead fruit and foliage.

But at least the bail of straw I'd spread among the plants wasn't a waste of time. I poured paraffin on it, chucked a match and the whole lot went up into a nice little bonfire.

I'll give 'em a miss next year ... probably.

Anyway, this mysterious millennium bug that everyone talked about,

And got worried about,
But it never came about,
I think I've figured out.
I reckon it came in the guise of blight …
… on my allotment anyway.

I'm going to grow Jerusalem artichokes next year for
the first time. I've looked it up and it seems you grow
'em in a similar way to potatoes. They grow
underground like a potato and in general you harvest
them like a potato and cook 'em like a potato. Kate likes
'em and wants Harry to taste 'em. I think Charlie will
like 'em too.

I'll let you know how they fared on the reprint if this
comes out before they do.

MULCHING AND RAMBLING

I mentioned 'mulching' a few paragraphs back when I said I used straw to 'mulch' my tomatoes. Mulching vegetables is a great idea for the rock 'n' roll gardener. It does two great things. It suppresses the weeds and stops the soil from drying out quickly. You can mulch with straw or compost, or both if you wish.

Runner beans, or French climbing beans, are a favourite mulch of mine. ('Mulch of Mine'. A lovely old forgotten song. Victorian men of the working class in crusty trousers would croon this tune together on gas-lit street corners in those days gone by.)

Mulching is a great way of giving young plants a good start and good support for the rest of their life. It's a lovely touch to sending them on their way.

Mulching is like seeing your favourite nephew off to boarding school. He's got everything he needs: Helix geometry set, trench coat and credit card. Then, just as the bus is leaving, you thrust a brown paper parcel into his arms. It's a nice pair of sturdy, comfortable boots so he'll have no trouble with his feet. They don't excite him much, but you know that so long as he wears them his feet will grow fit and healthy.

This is what mulching does; it looks after the 'feet' of the beans. Mulch after you've got the nice climbing plants growing well (at least six inches high) in among the smart bamboo canes. Do it when the plants are looking confident and ready for the climb. And each one wants to climb up that cane. Why? Because it's there. So they're sure gonna welcome that extra help from down below.

I use straw to mulch. I like the look and the smell of it.

(Sounds like a song? 'I'd Mulch the World with Straw, Just for the Hell of It'. Or how about, 'When You're Mulching' to the tune of 'When You're Smiling', or 'Whole Lotta Mulching Going On' or an Elvis number, 'Jailhouse Mulch' or 'Just let Me Be, Your Teddy Mulch' or Frank Sinatra, 'Mulch Me to the Moon' or ...).

(I have a lot more 'Mulch' song suggestions but have transferred them to the end of the book. Flip to the end or read on. Take note of the number of this page though.)

Well, before I actually mulch, I make sure there isn't a weed in sight. Then, around each plant, I carefully lay a two- or three-inch thick mulch of straw, filling the whole area to about a foot around the outside of the bean plot.

Do the same around everything if you can, making sure you've de-weeded first so that it's all getting a good start. Make sure the plants are big enough to rise above the straw.

You won't have to weed and water so much if you do this, so it's worth the effort 'cos ain't these the most tedious tasks?

Actually, they can be enjoyable once you settle into it, but they ain't the most enjoyable parts of vegetable gardening. It's a bit like plugging and promoting your record or book once it's out (well, not as bad as that). It has to be done or you ain't gonna harvest all you've sown. Or they ain't gonna hear all you've recorded. Or they ain't gonna read all you've written.

So it must all be done if you want taters on your plate or in the bank.

I must've already said in this book how good growing my own vegetables makes me feel - head and body. I love the open air and vegetable gardening is the perfect open-air activity for me. It's got everything going for it. Do it all at a steady pace and it'll keep you well fit. You won't have to go down to the gym.

"Hang on a minute!" you're probably saying. "How comes Chas is spouting off about keeping fit? Ain't he the tubby one?" Yes I was till I got the allotment (and cut down on potatoes). I ain't tubby no more. In any case I was never really that fat. It's only 'cos I sit down at the piano and on telly it makes me look like the short, fat one. But I'm taller than Dave. In fact he used to be known by my uncles and aunts as 'Little Dave'. Dave weren't none too pleased with this handle. But, to be fair, it was only 'cos I've got an older brother called Dave who is tall too. It was purely a case of differentiation that Dave got dubbed the titch. My brother was known as 'Big Dave' and mate Dave was known as 'Little Dave'. It's as simple as that.

So you see it all ties up very nicely, like protagonists in a Grimm's fairy tale. I like people to be clear about what they're dealing with and, of course, no paths will be put in until it's clearly seen where the people walk.

So, now my tubby days are over I don't want any more of the 'he's the short, fat cunt on the piano' if that's okay by you. Not that you ever did say it, but I'm making it a point, just in case.

Come down and have a look on my next gig. Have a look at the place where my fat belly used to be. That last sentence sounds like a Harry Champion song. Now there's a thought. A few years ago me and Dave could've gone out as 'Tubby and Titch'. What do you think about that?

I ain't gonna dwell on it, but the decade of the '90s was crap for me. I look back on it as a hiccup in my life, or a decade of trapped wind if you like. (Good name for an old boys' jazz band that: 'Trapped Wind.')

It sort of felt like if I could only let go one big, long fart, everything would be alright and I'd be able to pay off the mortgage. But life ain't so simple.

For some, so they say, maybe. But I've never yet spoken to anybody who can confirm it.

The one redeeming feature of that decade for me was Charlie, my granddaughter, born in 1994.

I didn't do much gardening. I didn't do much of anything other than gigging. The gigs were good and they kept me going, but just par for the course. Not like they are now.

No new Hungarian Rhapsody Rock or Burtie drum solo leg dancing.

I had settled for the bad habits and was enjoying them … I thought. Easily done. Bad habits click in overnight and you think, 'Who was it that said they were bad? I'm feeling pretty good sitting here in this pub.'

But I'm a late grower upper. I don't look back to when I was a kid and think, 'If only I knew then what I know now'. I look back to last Friday and think, 'If only I knew then what I know now'.

Am I joking? I don't even know. I think I am, but there are times when I'm not sure. And this is one of those times.

Hang on, I think I've sussed it. It's fifty-fifty. Part joke, part serious.

But I've well caught up with my proper 'today' self, and I'm enjoying it immensely, without the enjoyable bad habits. And there've been some.

Actually, I have now paid off my mortgage, but I am still waiting for that long fart. But I've a feeling I'll get there.

There've been a few short to medium trumps along the way that have assured me that I'm on the right path to 'farteousness'.

That day will come. Shit or bust.

Anyway, back to the plot …

Now what's the worst thing that can happen to a vegetable gardener?

The worst thing that can happen to a vegetable gardener is that those vegetables he has lovingly produced end up remaining uneaten. They either go to seed or they go rotten in the bottom of the fridge and get chucked out to be replaced by some plastic-covered, drugged-up, supermarket 'floozie veggie', all polished and shiny on the outside, but full of 'E' numbers and mystery on the inside.

(These vegetables are so potentially hyperactive that it ain't gonna be long before the security men in Sainsbury's will have their hands full chasing after turnips and parsnips running about in and out the aisles. Then just wait till the oven-ready chickens get wind of it. My muvver's good gawd.)

At last the 'organic' mode is considered 'non-cranky'. It was thought of like that in the '60s and '70s believe it or not. In fact I was a bit of a pioneer really. My kids got a bit of the taste of the good life. Organic in the shops is at last being seen more as the proper way forward.

But still, in the meantime, the only way to be sure is to grow your own. And, of course, for all time.

Once I've produced the vegetable babies on my allotment, my job is done. They are there for loving devouring, and to be swooned over 'cos the Queen don't eat none better.

Darling daughter Kate took full advantage of my produce while she was pregnant with Harry. He was a nice 10 pound 2 ounce baby, full of granddads spinach and parsnip via Kate.

He's 15 months old at the time of writing this (May 2009). Harry's first solid food was my carrot. As I sowed the seeds I was picturing Harry's first taste. Kate sent me a picture on my phone of Harry eating his first mashed carrot, grown by granddad. The smile on his face said it all.

My allotment is two minutes from Kate's, so Harry is growing up with plenty of grandpa's veg close at hand.

I wonder what he's going to call me?

Granddaughter Charlie's early interpretation of 'granddad' was 'panda'. It stuck.

My mum said I used to call my grandfather 'Gunfire'. Makes sense. Similar sound and the war was on.

Scrumping Tip...

If you ever go scrumping or get invited to pick and take home apples from someone's tree, for immediate consumption, pick the ones with a maggot hole in them. I kid you not. These will be the sweetest on the tree. The maggot ain't no fool. He's got good taste. He will nibble around. You will often see one tiny bite on an apple and no more. Don't touch this one, 'cos it will be sour. Either he's tried it or something else has and moved on. To find a sweet one, look for one with a deep maggot hole and you've found a sweet one. Just cut round him and the hole and you're in for a treat.

A couple of years ago on the allotment some serious vegetable scrumping started happening. Well, sort of serious. Potatoes had been dug and nicked from various plots (it was a rare blight-free year for us). I suppose about a sackful was scrumped from my plot, which was quite a lot really.

But I couldn't get that mad at the scrumpers. I knew what they were doing - knocking on people's houses and saying, "Sack of taters lady? A fiver?" Or whatever was a going cut-price rate at the time. The feeling I got was more one of being pleased that somebody was eating them and enjoying them. Vandalism would've made me mad, but not really tater scrumping.

But then I've got the luxury of not having to rely on my crops to feed my kids, ain't I? If the produce that I'd planned for my family's' survival had got stolen, then my feelings would've been different - very much so.

But whatever, it was getting to be a bit of a nuisance that summer. Every two or three days someone else's plot got done. So a vigilant plan was set up.

I first got to know about it when going home from my plot one evening at dusk. It was a nice late-summer evening and I'd been at the plot starting a bit of digging ready for the winter.

It was time to go home. As I walked past John's plot on the left there comes a quiet but positive voice: "G'night Charlie!" It startled me slightly. It seemed to come from right out of his runner beans. "G'night John, "I said. He's staying late, I thought. Strange.

I strolled on towards the gate. Nice evening. Then, "G'night Charlie!" I hear from the right. It was Albert. I recognised his voice coming from the region of his marigolds, their yellow petals just visible in the fading light. He grows 'em every year to keep the blackfly away from his runner beans. He don't get troubled. But then nor do I. Perhaps his marigolds keep 'em away from my plot too. He's only just the other side of the path. "G'night Albert," I said, and strolled on.

"G'night Charlie!" It was my Italian mate, Vito. His voice came from behind a wild, tousled (just visible in the dark) grapevine. "G'night Vito, 'night boys," I said as I reached the exit gate.

It was just like 'Dads Army' back there, I thought.

Then the penny began to drop.

They were all lying in wait and ready for any scrumpers, and not knowing from which direction they might come they were covering all areas.

"Need any help?" I shouted gently before I left. "No!" came the hushed reply.

There were no intruders that night and there haven't been any since. If there had been any I don't think there would've been any rough stuff. I think the boys would've frightened the life out of 'em with a few good old-style "Gertchas!" and sent 'em running.

HORSERADISH

Most people are familiar with horseradish sauce - jars you can buy in the supermarket to accompany the Sunday roast beef. And it's very good. But it ain't as good as the horseradish that used to accompany my granddads Sunday dinner. He grew it and made it himself. I used to ask him for a smell of it. "Be careful, boy," he'd say. Then I knew what he meant after a sniff. It was initially very pleasant and then it punched you on the nose.

It is actually very similar to getting kicked in the bollocks. Let me explain, for the ladies, who have no such things. But wait awhile. The more I think about it, probably the only similarity is the delayed effect? No. That's not good enough.

I've dug a hole for myself so it's up to me to get out of it.

When you get kicked in the bollocks, it hurts - but initially it just hurts, like a kick in the side, or a kick in the leg, or a kick in the thigh. But with a kick in the side, leg or thigh you get the worst pain on impact and it lingers but it finally begins to subside. With a kick in the bollocks (I kid you not, ladies) you get the initial pain on impact but then ten seconds later it's fuckin' murder! When you see a footballer rolling about on the pitch after one of them, he ain't acting. It's like a sudden attack of gastro-enteritis in your crutch minus the shits.

So. How's this similar to horseradish? You got me thinking now.

Oh yeah. It's the delayed effect. But there is a difference. Horseradish: sniff – lovely; seconds later - wallop! - punch on the nose. Kick in the bollocks: hurts;

seconds later – fucking hurts.

Another analogy could be (this one's clean and could make a good TV ad):

'It's rock 'n' roll slap back echo in a jar. It makes you wanna throw back your head and holler like Little Richard!'

My granddad used to put vinegar on everything. I'm sort of like that now, and so is my granddaughter Charlie. It's lovely stuff. If granddad left anything on his plate, greens or potatoes, with vinegar, I'd be in there finishing it off.

One Sunday afternoon I spotted a nice beef meatball he'd left. That's for me! Bound to have some nice granddad vinegar on it. There was. But after a few seconds of chewing it dawned on me that this had been chewed before, but it was too tough so granddad had spit it out and left it on the side of his plate. Now just forget what I've just said or you won't want to know what went into granddads Sunday dinner horseradish.

Granddads roast beef accompaniment was just fresh grated or minced horseradish and malt vinegar. That's all. I've got some in the fridge now. I ate some with a sirloin steak a couple of hours ago and I might have some more with a bit of boiled bacon before bedtime. Well, I feel like that now, but I might say fuck it, I'm going to bed. I don't like making rigid plans.

Horseradish grows wild everywhere. Look out of the window on your next railway journey. What you might think are dock leaves (large spear-like leaves) growing alongside the tracks are more than probably ... no, most likely ... no, most definitely horseradish.

It's found on every allotment, not actually on the plots but beside them. Let it get on your plot and it'll take over. It's extremely deep rooted and it's the root that you eat. You can't dig up a whole root like you can with a carrot or parsnip, as they're too deep. You can only dig up part of it, but that don't matter. Part of it is enough. An old boy once told me that the roots can go down ten feet. I thought he was exaggerating at the time, but I ain't so sure now. I ain't ever been able to dig out a whole root of it. You just dig up biggish knobbly bits. In fact don't even try to dig up a whole root of it. You'll break your fork. It's easily done. I've done it.

But it really is worth all the effort.

Clean what knobbly bits you can with a potato peeler and then you can grate it, but the best way is to mince it. Do it outside if you can. It really goes for you if you mince or grate it indoors. It acts like a nasty dog. It makes you think there's got to be a way of putting a muzzle on it. Preparing onions ain't in the same league as horseradish. You start indoors and you think, 'What's all the fuss about?' Then before you know it - wallop! It's got your ankle this time and you're out on the dance floor on one leg hollering, again, like Little Richard.

After you've recovered, put it in a jam jar and top it up with malt vinegar. It keeps for ages in the fridge.

Stanley Mills, our publisher in New York, is mad for it. We invite him to dinner when he comes over. He said how his mother would love it as she'd lost her sense of taste for most things. I sent him some through the post. Stanley said she tasted that alright!

I got my son Nik to post the package. "What's this, dad? New songs for the American market?"

"No, horseradish."

"'Oh well. That's my dad."

MINT, MINT SAUCE AND CATS AND DOGS

My favourite Sunday roast is roast lamb, and mint sauce is the traditional accompaniment.

I must've eaten hundreds of roast lamb dinners on the road over the years in all sorts of restaurants, from pub grub to multiple-starred, top-class establishments. In general I've had some great roast lamb in most of these places, but in all of these places bar one I've had crap mint sauce.

Whether it be the suited, bow-tied, well-schooled waiter, or the young, pretty Essex girl with her hair in tufts, when mint sauce is called for, up it comes, exactly the same: out of a jar or bottle, devoid of flavour, but with a strange smell of TCP (that some big company food taster deemed to be 'mint flavour').

Neither 'Bow Tie' nor 'Pretty Tufty Hair' apologises with, "Sorry, we have no fresh," 'cos neither of them know that serving such a thing is possible. They don't know how easy it is to produce fresh mint sauce. But then why should they? It's not their restaurant. It's he who runs it that should be ashamed of himself.

It's a complete mystery to me that over all the years that I've sat and had hundreds of roast lamb dinners I can only recall one occasion, in a hotel (it was in the Midlands and I'm ashamed to say I can't remember the name - I must've been so overwhelmed), that the mint sauce was fresh.

Ain't that a terrible average though? Fresh mint sauce is like fresh horseradish (only it don't punch you on the nose!) - once tasted, never forgotten. You'll never tolerate the bottled, jellied, whatever, medical-smelling crap again.

Fresh mint sauce ain't a Little Richard 'Ooh My Soul' horseradish hollering screamer. It's more of a Buddy Holly 'Listen to Me', mellow, mouth-watering, tasteful charmer. Both different, but both classics.

Now here's how easy it is to grow mint and make mint sauce.

Growing...

Don't fuck about growing it from seed. Not that growing stuff from seed is fucking about, but as far as mint is concerned it is. This is a much quicker and better way.

If you know somebody who has an established mint patch growing, then ask them to dig you up a root, a 'clod' if you like, about six inches in diameter. They'll be only too pleased. (If you don't know anybody, there's another alternative coming up later.) Once mint is established it can take over the whole garden, so they won't mind parting with a clod/clump or two.

Check that you like the variety first. There are many. Pick a leaf and rub it between your thumb and finger. Sniff it. If it makes your mouth water then it's the one.

Then just dig a hole, plonk in the clump, cover the roots with soil, water it in and let it go. Actually, it ain't a bad idea to plant it in a large container like an old tin bath or a large flowerpot. You can keep better control of it this way.

It will grow like a weed. Only this weed will give your taste buds endless pleasure. You will have a tasty mint patch for the rest of your life, and your kids' and your grandkids'.

In 1999 I was visiting my old schoolteacher, Miss McSweeny, in Edmonton. She's 91 now (2009) and still lively. She showed me the local newspaper and said it had a feature on our old school, Eldon Road. The school was built in 1899 and it was having its centenary celebrations, and there were letters in the article from old pupils of the school. Among them was a letter from Annie Spenceley. She was a school chum of my mum's. They were in the same class at Eldon Road in the 1920s. She lived in the next road to ours, but our back garden backed onto theirs, so we got to know 'em, like you do. You knew everyone in your own street in those days, plus one family in the next street whose garden backed onto yours.

So I went round to see her and it was a pleasant afternoon. She told me stories about her friendship with my mum in infant school and I said I'd like to go out into her garden, the one that overlooked mine when I was a kid. "I'm not a gardener!" she said, "but I'm happy with what's growing. It suits me."

So we went out. Three-quarters of her garden was mint! Lovely! On picking a leaf it smelt just like the variety my granddad used to grow. Then it dawned on me that it was the same variety. Sixty years ago granddad had planted a nice clump of mint just over the other side of the fence. The mint had spread, like mint does, and crept under the fence and here it was.

My only regret is that I didn't ask for a root. I planned to go back, but I never did.

If you don't know anybody with a mint patch, get a pot from a garden centre or, better still, a supermarket. It will be cheaper and just as good. Treat it the same way. Dig a hole, plonk in the clump, cover the roots, water it in and let it go.

If you spot any 'Bowles' mint on your garden centre rounds, get it. You won't be sorry. It's reckoned to be the mint for the 'epicure' (food connoisseur). I'll go along with that. I reckon it's the best for mint sauce. My old gardener's wife made mint wine from this variety and that was very tasty too. It was him that gave me the original clump of it.

Apart from the mint patch, my granddad didn't grow any edible crops in our old back garden. He grew potatoes on his allotment as I remember, but he was really more of a flower grower. Carnations were his speciality on the allotment. He grew gypsophila too - those tiny, delicate, white blooms you see in wedding bouquets. I think the Americans call it 'Babies Breath'.

A nice Sunday dinnertime memory was granddad biking up the pub with two or three bunches of white carnations on the handlebars. What a lovely smell. They would well pay for his beer. He would bunch together 10 or 20 stems to look like one massive bloom.

It's only the white carnations that smell. I don't know why. Perhaps I'll find out one of these days. But there isn't an answer to every question and I might have to settle for that.

Granddad took me over to his allotment a couple of times, but to be honest I don't know why. He never asked me to do anything and he never showed me how to grow anything. I would busy myself scrumping goosegogs from his mate's plot.

But granddad wasn't really interested in his grandkids like I am. I'm not saying he didn't love us in his own way, it's just that he was a 'roll a fag, fart, and do the pools' type of granddad. He probably didn't realise it, and I only just have, that these three things were 'do something I like, do something that makes me feel better, and do something that might make me rich'.

Kids seemed to be only handy for running errands. That's how he was brought up, I suppose. You would get 3d (1p) if you went round the corner to get his tobacco. My mate Reggie Hawkins, early Outlaws band member and still a musician mate now, remembers coming round my house when were teenagers. We had a gig at the King's Head and he came round to give me a hand up Town Road with my new bass amp. I wasn't quite ready to go, so granddad got Reggie to go round the corner for his tobacco. He gave him 3d. Granddad's money head never got beyond the First World War.

Granddad was a First World War survivor. It must've been heaven to be able to experience simple pleasures like rolling a fag, farting and doing the pools knowing that the immediate future didn't hold the probability of being blown up or shot.

Now I said that granddad didn't grow any edible crops, apart from mint, in our back garden, but mum said he did grow marrows on top of our World War II Anderson shelter.

My dad wasn't a gardener, but he had plenty of other traits in common with my mum - a sense of humour for one. My mum would get nervous in the air raids.

"Don't worry!" said my dad. "We're all going to be given brand new air raid shelters soon. And these are special ones. They can jump out of the way of the bombs. The only trouble is, you get in it at the bottom of your garden in Edmonton, but when you get out you're in Ponders End."

Larry (the sweet pea 'pee' man) dug up the old Anderson shelter in 1949. I remember him doing it. I was five. Granddad put a door on it and it became his garden shed. I was intrigued by the hinges. He'd cut up an old leather belt and nailed sections of it from door to post. I've never seen hinges like it before or since. He wasn't an inventive man. Perhaps he'd seen this done on makeshift officers' quarters in the trenches. Just a guess.

The back garden had a laburnum tree on one side and a rowan tree on the other, with the dug-up Anderson shelter at the end. Another early memory was of Cosmos sown by mum. It's a tall, slender, graceful, daisy-like flower of various colours, with slender fern-like leaves. I thought it was amazing that they appeared again the year after without mum doing anything - an observation that sparked an early gardening interest. They had seeded themselves, of course.

It's easy to figure out why most of the memories of the past remain with you, but that ain't so with all of them. I remember, with the help of my mum, growing my first lettuces at the bottom of that garden. They tasted wonderful. I ate them when they were about four inches high. I couldn't wait. I had them between slices of bread with salad cream. I could just eat one now.

Now it's easy to figure out why I remember that one. But why do I remember this one? I'm stumped.

I was about nine. There was nan, one afternoon, standing by the kitchen door looking out towards the back garden. She had a proud look on her face, like a mum might have on parents' day on seeing her son being presented with a special award.

"What you looking at, nan?" I asked.

"Shush," she said softly. "Look, it's Vick. He's having a crap."

'Crap'? This was a new word on me. But on looking at Vick, I saw he was having a shit. I soon put two and two together. She continued looking at Vick, with a serene, calm, contented look on her face. She didn't look at me. She kept her eyes on Vick. I felt the need to say nothing. I didn't want to interrupt. She spoke to me softly, but her mind was on Vick. Looking back, perhaps Vick had been having a bit of trouble and seemed to be now, at last, getting back onto the road of regularity? It's always worrying, that sort of thing.

But then, how would she know if he was regular or not? You couldn't keep track of him all the time. He could be shitting regular without you knowing. Well couldn't he? How would she know? Cats ain't like dogs. They come and go and do as they please. You never know what they're up to.

But it was the first time I'd ever heard the word 'crap' and nan was looking at Vick having one.

We all said 'shit' in the street, but not indoors. Perhaps that's why it sticks in my mind? This new word, 'crap'?

It actually describes the function very well, especially a cat's, 'cos all sorts of 'snap, crackle and pop' or 'crap and bang' noises like a toy cap gun come from its arse while it strains one out. 'Bap! Bap! Bap! Bap! ... Razzo ... Tap! Bang! Pop! ...' There you are then.

One Saturday night, or probably early Sunday morning, when I was a teenager, I got woken up from a snooze on the front room floor by one of my mum's cats straining one out close by my ear. It had the cheek to stare at me indignantly while it was doing it. I still remember the noise. It started off like a speeded-up chainsaw misfiring. This went on for a while - accompanied by mighty big stink, I might add. Finally it all came to end with a noise sounding like an enormous dreg of water being sucked down the plughole. It stared me out throughout, with a look of 'who you looking at, cunt?'

Yes. Cats are noisy crappers. But it ain't so much the noise, it's more the tone range. The noise was enough to wake me up, but not the neighbours, as far as I know. Cats crap in a style that takes on a lot of different tones: medium low parps to high electrical sizzling sounds. Yes, there were sparks coming from that cat's arse that night, no doubt about it.

I remember telling this story to Ritchie Blackmore. He said it was probably getting its own back on me.

"What do you mean?" I said.

Then he went into one of his uncontrollable tear-filled giggles. I knew something 'turd- like' was on its way, like when he ... but that's another story.

"You do it," he said, looking me squarely in the eyes, mirthfully, "I do it whenever I can." Another semi-giggle fit. "I just know you do it. It's just the sort of thing you would do."

"What?!"

"Fart on the cat."

Feel a fart coming on and the cat is slumbering on the

sofa? Position your arse right above the cat's head and fart? Yes, he was right, I had done it - but only once or twice. Not as much as him I bet.

So yes, you will find, right here, the answer to one part of the blurb on the back cover of this book.

Question: 'What did Chas and Ritchie Blackmore both do that they kept secret from their mums?'

Answer: 'Fart on the family cat.'

Before I leave my early teenage memories of animal action at home with mum and family, Mitch the dog comes to mind. No, nobody would fart on him. Nobody would dare to. He would have your bollocks off.

He was a stray that mum took in. He was a sort of North London Welsh collie. He loved a party of a Saturday night, especially when couples got up to dance. Ankles were there for the biting. When he was on the streets in his younger days he'd obviously been kicked by feet that had ankles like that.

Pissed Irishmen (stepfather Irish John's mates) dancing in the old front room on a Saturday night and hollering "Fluten Hell!" now and then when their ankles got bit by Mitch was a normal scene in our house. Mitch loved them parties - plenty of ankles. The dancers would get slightly perturbed, but not much. There would be a mingling of chatting up crumpet, slow smooch dancing and the occasional holler/shout of pain. But as Mitch moved round to another ankle, all would be forgotten and they'd just carry on partying, only to remember and holler once again when Mitch came back for round two.

Mitch was a dog out there on his own. My mum was his one love, but if any of my mates came round and fell asleep in the armchair - like we've all been known to do - Mitch would guard him. Nobody but nobody would be allowed to wake him up or even touch him, not even my mum. Mitch would stand guard while he slept, even though he may have been a stranger to Mitch before that night. One move to wake him up and Mitch would have you. He did it to me. Harvey Hinsley, our guitar player, was round one night and fell asleep in the armchair. I went to wake him with a gentle pat of my hand. As I moved my arm towards Harvey, Mitch went for me. He didn't actually bite, but he would've done if I'd touched Harvey.

I've never known a dog like him.

And so back to Vick having a shit/crap in the garden.

Now that nan had used this new word 'crap' in such a casual way to me, I must've thought it reasonable to assume that I could say it indoors. I can't remember trying it though. I must've still been a bit wary. Or perhaps I did? Not sure.

I can only state that whenever I hear the word 'crap' today, I picture a cat's arse and all the rest of the bizzo, sparks 'n' all.

But it was that look of complete contentment on nan's face. That cat, having a crap, filled her heart with joy.

I never found out the reason why.

It will have to remain another one of the great mysteries of life.

Another unanswered question, like is there really a God?

If so, who made him? And if God made Father Christmas, how comes the kid down the end of the road got a bike and I only got a football bladder?

Before I leave the turd subject, I must draw your attention to the fact that dogs crap in a different style.

You take 'em for a walk, they get sniffing, and - boomp, boomp, boomp - they're away. Back arched, but silent. No snap, crackle or pop cap-gun sounds like them wonky cats, but proper silent dog turds.

I've often seen dogs being taken for a walk going into that arched back routine, leaving a brown berringer for its master to deal with. They don't care who's looking. My little border terrier Archie does 'em. I usually kick it into touch. Toe punt. 'Brown one, in the ditch. La-La La-La-La'.

But just imagine if people were like that. You're walking down a leafy lane with your boyfriend and suddenly he starts sniffing around and the next thing he's bandying his legs, arching his back and in a creeping crouch. Then - boomp, boomp, boomp -he's done it. Now he might have a face and body that melts your heart, but after that you'd have to finish with him, wouldn't you? No matter how he pleaded with you to see his side of it. No matter how he promised it wouldn't happen again. How it was only a one-off. It would sure be a difficult one.

For instance, you're invited to your best friend's wedding at a big country house. It's a lovely day and you're all on the lawn drinking champagne. Then you catch that look in his eye. His legs start to bandy and he passes you his glass. Oh no, he's off again, into that creeping crouch and all that goes with it. It's now beginning to be his natural, usual style of regularity. What's more, he don't even seem worried about it.

Just how are you going to deal with this sort of thing in the future?

It's a shame, I know, but I would say it's just too much of a risk to take. The next thing you know he'll be grabbing your leg and giving it humping movements.

You'll need to give it some serious thought.

Mint Sauce...
Pick a bunch of mint. Wash it and discard the tough stalks. Chop it pretty fine on a chopping board, with a level teaspoon of sugar sprinkled over it. (Adding the sugar at this stage soaks up the mint juice.)

Put it in a teacup-sized dish, sprinkle with salt and add straight from the kettle about a dessertspoon of boiling water. Then add two or three dessertspoons of malt vinegar. Do this about an hour before dinnertime and it will be ready in time for dinner.

There again, this mint sauce keeps well for a long time in a jam jar in the fridge.

If in the mood, and it's the sort of thing I do if I'm listening to a radio play, make enough to fill a few jam jars. You won't need to add boiling water this time, just add cold, as it will have plenty time to infuse. Make it about three-quarters vinegar and one-quarter water. You can also freeze it in ice cube trays if you want.

'CHASTYLE' COOKERY

Here are some recipes I've devised that have been well tested by me and also tested out on Dave.

A Chastew
If there was songwriting to be done for a new album, me and Dave would go away for a week or so to the country to get the job done. Going away to write not only produced good songs but also got me into how to cook a good stew. We both love stew and this is what we would live on for the whole period, topping it up every day.

It might start its life as a rabbit stew, for instance.

Ingredients:
1 rabbit
Assorted vegetables
2 stock cubes
Parsley

Method:
Preferably use a wild rabbit, as they taste better. Let the butcher prepare it. You can prepare it yourself, but they do pen and ink a bit. Tell him you want the kidneys. Rabbit kidneys are the best in the world. One of my early memories was offering the rabbit kidneys on my plate to my mum. I knew she loved them and she knew I did. I must've been about five. "No, Chas, I've had enough. You eat them." It was a nice thing for me to do at that age, wasn't it?

I could eat some right now. I keep doing that, don't I? Writing about food that I like and wishing I had some right now!

Have I mentioned rollmop herrings yet? Well, I've just had some. It's three in the morning and all is well. I will creep to bed at four. If I haven't mentioned *this* before, this is my normal routine.

Bed at four, up at noon. What a life! My dream when I was a youngster come true. Don't you envy me?

Anyway, back to the stew.

So, one prepared rabbit.

Bring it to the boil in salted water. There will be scum. Tip away the water and scum. Scrub its arse if there's any sticking to it.

Begin the stew. Add fresh water to just cover the rabbit and add whatever vegetables you've got: carrots, onions, peas, turnips, cabbage, in fact anything and everything. This is all part of the fun. Add some minced or chopped parsley if you can. It's very tasty and high in vitamin C. It gives it that 'pie and mash' shop liquor flavour. (The pots of parsley you get in the supermarket can also be planted out to grow on.)

Add a couple of stock cubes, any kind. You can mix 'em up - a chicken and a beef or whatever. Cover with water.

Bring to the boil, just, and put it in the bottom oven (slow oven). Let it go for at least two hours. It can be longer if you want. It won't spoil.

I'm talking Aga now. Like I said, everybody, no matter how big or small the house is, must make room for a piano and an Aga.

You won't regret it. You don't have to be a cook to use an Aga. You just open the oven door and put food in it. While it's busy cooking you can play the piano or learn to play it if you haven't done so already. Agas are the biz. For instance, if you want lamb chops just put them on the rack and shut the door for 20 minutes.

Make sure you've got a timing bibber! You're bound to forget.

You never have to clean out an Aga oven. I sound like an Aga salesman, don't I?!

But, whatever, any oven knows how to simmer a stew.

Then, in me and Dave's cottage, this rabbit stew was daily added to. Lamb chops the next day, bacon, leeks, peas, beans.

It begins to take on a flavour of its own. Everything I add seems to send it up a notch. I begin to think close on crazy. How about sell-by-date catgut bass strings? Or some old sun-dried banjo vellums? Or slightly used half-corona stogies? No. I drew the line at these. I wasn't going to push my luck. Take it easy, old son. Don't spoil it. Carry on doing what you're doing, but keep that thought behind it. Make sure, whatever you add, you actually like the taste of it, even though you've not had them all together in one dish. So that's what I did.

After a week (I should've written it down) it was impossible to work out what was actually in it. But was that important? It's cooking on jazz. With modern technology they probably could work it out. A DNA test might do it. Or sniffer dogs. Or one of them pregnancy testing kits. But I wasn't going to get into that.

The main thing was the taste, and in the first couple of days the initial daily additions were producing mighty good stew.

Then, on the third day, it began to take on a slight flavour of mud.

This had to be looked into. The daily augmented stew had 'done took an unexpected turn for the worse'. (For some reason those last few words that came into my head took on a sort of Deep South blues/gospel flavour. Why? Search me. They just did. Perhaps there is a God after all).

BUT THAT'S HOW THEY COOKED STEWS IN SHAKESPEARE'S TIME, ISN'T IT?

That's where I got the idea from.

I done the tour in Stratford-upon-Avon …

At his house …

Where they show you the square wooden 'trencher' plates that they ate off and tell you that that's where 'a square meal' came from. That's what they said. And the stew. They added to the pot every day. That's where the term 'pot luck' came from.

"What's for dinner Ma?"

"It's in the pot. Take pot luck."

But when Shakespeare took 'pot luck' did he really say, "Bollocks! I'm not eating that. I'll have the shits for a week. Can't you think of a better way of cooking a stew? Fuck this 'pot luck' lark. I'm going down to the Strumpets Thigh and have some wench cheese and bogey bread. Pot luck? Stick it up your arse!"

And out he goes, slamming the door. Fucking good riddance I say. Cocky little cunt.

But back to the subject of the 'pot luck' stew.

Something wasn't ringing true with this historical recipe, so I decided history had to be rewritten proper - without the lawyers' favourite term, the old BS ('bullshit' for those who ain't initiated. They cleverly think of ways they can use it. If they're on your side it's handy.)

You see, Shakespeare's kids wouldn't have stood for such a daily 'pot luck' dinner. I know. (Did he have kids? Don't matter.) I've got kids of my own. No good saying, "It's good for you!" Why do we keep saying this? It never has worked. But our kids will say the same to their kids and so it will go on. While I'm at it, when you say, "That's the best part!" when your kids won't eat their bread crusts, that don't work either. But it ensures that they'll say it to their kids and theirs to theirs.

This is what I reckon the Shakespeare stew cookers really did. They didn't keep continually adding to it. After every couple of days, they ate it all and started again.

I followed a similar plan for me and Dave and it

worked well.

But today, if you've got a freezer, wonderful things can be done. I'm going to give you a plan based on the old (supposed) idea, without the mud.

Now listen here. This works well. Log this plan in your diary. You won't do it if you don't, 'cos it's near impossible to memorise. Just check your diary on a daily basis as to what has to be done. It's simple that way. But do do it, 'cos it's worth it. Don't question it, just follow it. Like you do your sat-nav. Well, Dave don't.

"Take the first exit," says 'Jane'.

"That ain't the way," says Dave, who's got the worst sense of direction in the world. "It's up here."

And Dave goes for the second exit.

"What the fuck we got a sat-nav for if we're going to ignore it?" says I.

But I let him have his head. Then, when hopelessly lost, 'Jane' takes over and we find the gig.

So follow this route as it is writ, then once you get the general idea you can start planning your route from A to Z in your own style.

On the first day (get your diary, find 'Monday' and begin making notes), cook the stew as per rabbit stew (see back yonder). Cook a fairly big one - enough for two days with some left over. Freeze what's left over.

On the third day, cook another one. This time it might be beef, for instance. Make the same quantity - enough for two days. Freeze what's left over.

On the fifth day, lamb and same again.

On the seventh day, boiled bacon most probably.

Then, on the eighth day, let there be no cookery.

Make sure you've frozen the quantities in small portions, a portion being about the size of a piece of horse dung that the coalman's horse would do in days gone by, and that you would pick up and throw at your mate. It's the only thing I could think of that is smaller than a tennis ball and bigger than a golf ball. Now here comes the tasty, fun and 'pot luck' bit without the Shakespeare mud.

On the eighth day, take as many random small quantities out of the freezer that you can eat that day. It might be two rabbit, one lamb and one bacon, or whatever. Put 'em all in a pot until they're hot.

Pot luck, no mud and very tasty!

Do the same with the frozen stews for the rest of the week. If you do happen to run out by the end of the week, go out for an Indian.

Start up again the week after. You will be eating well this way. Nothing goes down the sink. All the juices from the vegetables and meat stay trapped in the stew. I know technically a stew cooked in the oven is called a casserole, but the word 'stew' sounds tastier.

So that's the Chastew.

I mentioned earlier about using as a fun missile a handy knob of horse dung. I remember hitting Ernie Mortimer a smart one on the back of the head with one. I loved throwing things like this at other kids, especially when they weren't looking. Not bricks or painful things but horse dung or apple cores.

I love apples. Even today when I finish an apple I immediately look around for a handy back of neck I can chuck the core at like I used to in the playground. The worst of it is, the last time I finished one the back of neck I saw was the old gel over the road pruning her roses.

The trick at school was to chuck the apple, hit the back of neck, then immediately engross yourself in your tasty cold toast lunch. It was particularly good to watch out of the side of your eye to see if he picked on someone else as the culprit and they began to have a bundle over it.

Anything else out of the ordinary that's tasty?

But of course!

Pigs' Trotters

I would say there ain't no better food in the world. My kids hate 'em. My son-in-law Paul said that when he first smelt me a-cooking 'em he pictured the kitchen of that serial killers kitchen who cooked his victims' body parts and flushed them down the lav. He reckoned it would've been a similar smell. But don't be put off by that.

I first tasted 'em hot. I still remember that taste. Lovely. My nan was a great one for coming in from the kitchen with a dish of something and saying, "Taste that." I wasn't one of those irksome kids who'd say, "What is it?" Nan brought it in with a 'you just wait till you do' look on her face, so I did. She did the same thing with pickled walnuts. I love them too. She knew my taste. She would buy me apples from Edmonton Green market – Bramley's cooking apples. I loved 'em raw. The added flavour of onions and potato mud that they mixed with in nan's shopping bag gave them unique class - something that's being missed today. You don't get proper-smelling, used shopping bags. Shopping bags have no smell. They should smell of onions and apples and the earth of potatoes, carrots and turnips and all such things. That is a proper shopping bag – like my nan's.

Nan was born in the latter part of the Victorian era and was brought up in Clerkenwell. It wasn't a really poor family, but they needed to spend every penny extremely wisely. They, and the families around her, ate well. But only just. She remembered it to be a rule that whenever her or her family were invited to dinner at anybody else's house (and it was the general rule), no matter how hungry they were they should leave a small piece of everything that was given to them on the plate. For instance, if the meal served was roast beef, Yorkshire pudding, Brussels sprouts, two kinds of potatoes and carrots, then a tiny piece of each was left. This said to the host, 'You have given me just enough of everything.' In my nan's day this was the done thing. The host had no need to ask if you wanted more, whether they had more to offer or not. Mostly they didn't.

In these days of plenty, it's hard to imagine actual starvation. I've been near that path, but thank fuck not actually on it.

Now why do I and a lot of us say 'thank fuck' for a lot of things? Did God create the world or did Fuck create the world? I ain't saying nothing.

So right, here we go. Pigs' Trotters. My brother Dave reckons they are better than jellied eels.

Ingredients:
2 pigs' trotters (the butcher will look at you in wonderment and then either give 'em to you for free or charge you 20 or 30 pence if you haven't bought anything else)
1 garlic clove
Pepper and salt
1 onion
1 bay leaf

Method:
Boil the trotters in salt water for five minutes. Tip away the water and scum. Rinse the trotters under the tap.

Put the trotters in a saucepan and cover with water. Add the other ingredients, the onion and garlic whole. Bring to the boil and simmer gently for two to three hours.

Remove the garlic, onion and bay leaf. Remove the bones and give 'em to the dog. Put the rest in a dish and put in the fridge.

When it's cold, season it with pepper and vinegar and eat it with dry bread.

You will be disappointed.

Disappointed that you only cooked two. You will definitely cook at least four next time.

So my brother Dave reckons they are better than jellied eels. It's nice that he says it and I know what he means. They are eaten in the same style and feeling - crusty dry bread and pepper and vinegar.

But my guess is, if the two dishes were put in front of him round my house after a couple or three pints down the pub, he'd go for the eels first. I ain't saying he wouldn't eat the trotters. I reckon he'd sit back and say, "Them eels were fucking lovely. Pass the vinegar and pepper. I'll have them trotters now."

Were the trotters a close second? Or was he saving the best till last? Whatever, there ain't much in it.

Finally, here's a recipe from my wife. It's for a beef pot roast that she did only last week. It really was tasty. I asked her how she did it, so here she is to tell you herself. Joan was a bunny girl in the sixties and she still looks as tasty today.

"I bought a brisket of beef weighing about a pound and in a cast-iron casserole dish (sturdy saucepan) I put a tablespoon of olive oil and put it on the simmering plate of the Aga for a few seconds to get hot. Then I seared (quick fried) the beef on all sides, just a few seconds a side. Then I added chopped onion, celery, carrots and swedes. In fact you can add whatever root vegetables you want and pack it all round the beef brisket. Next I added a full wine glass of beef stock seasoned with a couple of turns from the black pepper pot.

Then with the lid on I put it in the top oven for 20 minutes and in the simmering oven for two to three hours. Then I removed the meat from the casserole dish, put it on a plate on its own, and put it back in the bottom oven. Then I did the same with the vegetables. I removed them from the casserole dish and put them on their own, on a plate, in the bottom oven.

Finally, I skimmed the fat off the remaining gravy and rubbed it all over my body."

She didn't actually say that last bit. The vision just came to me as she told the story. What she actually said was:

"Finally, I mixed a dessertspoon of Bisto into a little cold water and added it to the gravy juices.

EPILOGUE

So, my dears, this is what I get up to food-wise: growing and cooking and other semi-related things in between.

Here's hoping you've enjoyed reading all about it and have gained inspiration and, like me, have had fun now and then, with the notion that there's plenty more of that and everything in life to come.

Last word:

Little but often in whatever you do and you won't go far wrong, chums, and if every now and then you feel like doing a lot, do it. It can be fun. But mostly keep to the little and often routine. The worst habit to get into is 'a lot and fuck all'. That ain't no good at all … to anyone.

Don't let the weeds take over. Keep your hoe with you at all times, knocking their heads off as you go. They'll get fed up in the end.

Happy growing days.

Time for bed. I've got to be up at the crack of noon.

MULCHING SONGS...

Cliff Richard, 'Livin' Mulch'; Elton John, 'Candle in the Mulch'; Jerry Lee Lewis, 'Lovin' Up a Mulch'; Paul McCartney, 'Mulch of Kintyre'; Rod Stewart, 'Maggie Mulch'; Elvis (again), 'Baby I Don't Mulch'; Lonnie Donegan, 'Don't You Mulch Me Daddy-O' or 'Bring a Little Mulch, Sylvie' or 'Cumberland Mulch'; Little Richard, 'I Can't Believe You Wanna Mulch'; Fats Domino, 'Blueberry Mulch'; Bobby Darin, 'Jack the Mulch'; Flatt and Scruggs, 'Beverley Mulch Billys'; Buddy Holly, 'Peggy Mulch' or 'That'll Be the Mulch' or the follow-up 'Peggy Mulch Got Married'; Bob Dylan, 'Blowing in the Mulch'; Barry Manilow, 'I Don't Wanna Mulch Without You Baby'; Deep Purple, 'Mulch on the Water'; Bill Haley, 'Shake Rattle and Mulch'; Hank Williams, 'Mulch Sick Blues' or 'Your Cheatin' Mulch'; James Brown, 'Cold Mulch'; The Beatles, 'All You Need is Mulch'; Gene Kelly, 'Singing in the Mulch'; Paul Robeson, 'Ol' Man Mulch'; Al Martino, 'Here in My Mulch' or 'Mulch Up Mother Brown'; The Everly Brothers, 'All I Have to Do is Mulch'; Ray Charles, 'Tell Me What I Mulch'; Wilson Pickett, 'In the Midnight Mulch' or '6 3 4 5 7 8 Mulch'; Chubby Checker, 'Let's Mulch Again Like We Did Last Summer'; Guy Mitchell, 'There's a Mulch Shop on the Corner in Pittsburgh Pennsylvania'; Gerry and the Pacemakers, 'You'll Never Mulch Alone'; Cliff Richard, 'Mistletoe and Mulch'; Frank Sinatra, 'New Mulch, New Mulch'; Bernard Cribbins, 'Mulch Said Fred'; Glen Campbell, 'Rhinestone Mulchboy'; Gerard Kenny, 'New Mulch, New Mulch, So Good They Mulched It Twice' ...
Happy Mulching!

NOTES:

NOTES:

NOTES:

NOTES:

NOTES:

NOTES:

www.apexpublishing.co.uk